I0037585

Personal Finance Terms

Financial Education Is Your Best Investment

Published March 18, 2019

Revision 2.1

Financial Terms Dictionary

Copyright And Trademark Notices

Limits of Liability and Disclaimer of Warranties

The materials in this book are provided "as is" and without warranties of any kind either express or implied. The Author disclaims all warranties, express or implied, including, but not limited to, implied warranties of merchantability and fitness for a particular purpose.

The Author does not warrant that defects will be corrected, or that that the site or the server that makes this eBook available are free of viruses or other harmful components. The Author does not warrant or make any representations regarding the use or the results of the use of the materials in this book in terms of their correctness, accuracy, reliability, or otherwise. Applicable law may not allow the exclusion of implied warranties, so the above exclusion may not apply to you.

Under no circumstances, including, but not limited to, negligence, shall the Author be liable for any special or consequential damages that result from the use of, or the inability to use this eBook, even if the Author or his authorized representative has been advised of the possibility of such damages.

Applicable law may not allow the limitation or exclusion of liability or incidental or consequential damages, so the above limitation or exclusion may not apply to you. In no event shall the Author's total liability to you for all damages, losses, and causes of action (whether in contract, tort, including but not limited to, negligence or otherwise) exceed the amount paid by you, if any, for this eBook.

Facts and information are believed to be accurate at the time they were placed in this book. All data provided in this book is to be used for information purposes only. The information contained within is not intended to provide specific legal, financial or tax advice, or any other advice whatsoever, for any individual or company and should not be relied upon in that regard. The services described are only offered in jurisdictions where they may be legally offered. Information provided is not all-inclusive and is limited to information that is made available and such information should not be relied upon as all-inclusive or accurate.

You are advised to do your own due diligence when it comes to making business decisions and should use caution and seek the advice of qualified professionals. You should check with your accountant, lawyer, or professional advisor, before acting on this or any information. You may not consider any examples, documents, or other content in this eBook or otherwise provided by the Author to be the equivalent of professional advice.

The Author assumes no responsibility for any losses or damages resulting from your use of any link, information, or opportunity contained in this book or within any other information disclosed by the author in any form whatsoever.

About the Author

Thomas Herold is a successful entrepreneur, mediator, author, and personal development coach. He published over 20 books with over 200,000 copies distributed worldwide and the founder of seven online businesses.

For over ten years Thomas Herold has studied the monetary system and has experienced some profound insights on how money and wealth are related. After three years of successful investing in silver, he released 'Building Wealth with Silver - How to Profit From The Biggest Wealth Transfer in History' in 2012. One of the first books that illustrate in a remarkable, simple way the monetary system and its consequences.

He is the founder and CEO of the 'Financial Terms Dictionary' book series and website, which explains in detail and comprehensive form over 1000 financial terms. In his financial book series, he informs in detail and with practical examples all aspects of the financial sector. His educational materials are designed to help people get started with financial education.

In his 2018 released book 'The Money Deception', Mr. Herold provides the most sophisticated insight and shocking details about the current monetary system. Never before has the massive manipulation of money caused so much economic inequality in the world. In spite of these frightening facts, 'The Money Deception' also provides remarkable and simple solutions to create abundance for all people, and it's a must read if you want to survive the global monetary transformation that's underway right now.

In 2019 he released an entirely new financial book series explaining in detail and with practical examples over 1000 financial terms. The 'Herold Financial IQ Series' contains currently of 15 titles covering every category of the financial market.

For more information please visit:

Herold Financial IQ Series

Herold Financial IQ Series

There are 15 books in this financial terms series available. Click the link below to see an overview and available formats available on Amazon.

Financial IQ Series on Amazon

Please leave your review on Amazon

This book and the Financial IQ Series is self-published and the author does not have a contract with one of the five largest publishers, which are able to support the author's work with advertising. If you like this book, please consider leaving a solid 5-star review on Amazon.

Financial IQ Series on Amazon

Table Of Contents

1035 Exchange

A 1035 Exchange is an exchange process that permits individuals to replace their existing life insurance policy or annuity contract with a similar new contract or policy. Thanks to a provision in the tax code, this can be affected without suffering any negative tax repercussions as part of the trade off exchange. The Internal Revenue Service permits those who hold these kinds of contracts to update their old policies and annuities with those more modern ones that include better benefits, superior investment choices, and lower fees.

The 1035 Exchange is also called a Section 1035 Exchange after the tax code section for which it is named. It literally permits policyholders to transfer their funds out of an endowment, life insurance policy, or annuity into a newer similar vehicle. The way it works is to allow holders to defer their gains. When all of the received proceeds of the original contract become transferred to the newer contract (as there are simultaneously not any loans outstanding on the prior policy), no tax becomes due at point of exchange. Should these proceeds be received and not exchanged according to the 1035 Exchange rules, then all gains obtained out of the first contract become taxable like ordinary income, and not as capital gains.

Gains do not refer to all money received. Instead they are the result of subtracting the gross cash value from the premium tax basis. This basis refers to the original dollar amount put into the contract itself minus the premiums paid for extra benefits or any distributions which qualify as tax free.

In order for this 1035 Exchange to make sense, it has to benefit the policy holder either economically or personally. It is also important for holders to never terminate their in place insurance policies until the newer policy has been fully issued and becomes effective. The holders need to contemplate any health changes since the original policy started. It might cost extra premiums in order for the newer policy to cover them. They might even receive a denial of coverage if the changes in health are too drastic. Similarly, if the holder is well advanced in age, the premium rate may increase.

Some policies also have surrender charges that must be considered. There may be different guarantees, provisions, and interest crediting in the newer policy as well. Most importantly, benefits of the newer policy have to be carefully reviewed. These may change negatively in some cases.

There are rare cases where simply surrendering an existing insurance policy or annuity is more advantageous than engaging in a 1035 Exchange. These primarily occur when the existing contract offers no gain. Sometimes outstanding loans on the initial policy also decrease the benefits of an exchange. In other cases, the original policy may have a "market rate adjustment" type of provision. This would cause the exchange proceeds to be less than those offered in a surrender.

It is usually the case that such a 1035 Exchange will be slower and more involved than simply surrendering the holder's original policy. It can even require a few months much of the time. This is why the conditions that affect the practicality of the exchange include financial conditions of the initial policy carrier, the country's economic climate at the time, and the intentions of the policy holder.

The IRS only deems certain exchanges to be considered "like kind" and allowable. These include life insurance for life insurance, life insurance for non-qualified annuity, life insurance for endowment, endowment for non-qualified annuity, endowment for endowment, and non-qualified annuity for non-qualified annuity. They also will allow multiple numbers of existing contracts to be changed into a single newer contract. It does not work in reverse. A single existing contract can not be exchanged in for multiple newer contracts, per the IRS rules and regulations.

401(k) Plan

401k retirement plans are specific kinds of accounts that the government established to help individuals to plan and save for retirement. Individuals fund these accounts using pre-taxed dollars from payrolls.

People invest money in these accounts into several different types of investments. These include stocks, mutual funds, and bonds. Gains earned in the account include dividends, capital gains, and interest. These gains do not get taxed until the owners withdraw the funds.

The name of the 401k comes from the portion of Internal Revenue Service Code which pertains to it. This vehicle for saving for retirement began in 1981 when an act of Congress created it.

There are a number of benefits to 401k accounts that recommend them to individuals. Five of these include tax benefits, flexibility of investments, employer matching programs, loan abilities, and portability.

The advantageous tax benefits are one of the main reasons that 401k plans are so popular. Money contributed does not become taxable until individuals withdraw it. Similarly gains accrued in the account are also tax-deferred. Over several decades, this makes a significant difference in the amount of money that people can save.

Investments that the IRS allows in these 401k retirement plans provide some flexibility. Those who do not want to take on much risk can choose to put more of their funds into shorter term bonds which are lower risk. Others who are more concerned with developing wealth over the long term can put a larger percentage of the money into equities like stocks and mutual funds. Company stock can also be acquired at a discount with many employers.

A tremendous edge that these 401k retirement plans provide their owners is the employer match feature. A great number of employers match their employees' contributions as a company benefit. This is done on a percentage basis. Newer employees may receive a 25% of contributions match, while employees who have been at a company longer may receive 50% or even 100% matches. Matches are only made on a certain maximum percentage of income that an employee contributes. This is the closest thing to free money a person can obtain at work.

Loan abilities from 401k retirements are a helpful feature for individuals in times of need. When people find themselves needing money with no other place to turn, the government permits them to obtain 401k loans from the plan. The plan administrator has to approve it as well. Loans from 401k plans are not taxed or penalized so long as they are repaid according to the repayment schedule and terms.

There are no restrictions on the uses of such loans. Some employers have minimum amounts that can be borrowed of $1,000 and a maximum number of loans an employee can take at a time. Sometimes employees will have to get their spouse's written consent before the company will issue the loan.

There are limits on the amount of a balance that can be borrowed. This is typically as much as 50% of the vested balance to no more than $50,000. When an employer will not allow an employee to take out a loan against the plan, hardship withdrawals can be requested. These are taxed and also penalized at a 10% rate.

Portability means the 401k retirement plan can go with the employees as they change jobs. Investors have four different choices for their 401k plan when they move to another company. They can choose to leave the plan with the old employer and pay any administration fees for the account staying there. They might instead do a rollover of their account to the new employer's 401k retirement plan.

A third option is to convert the 401k retirement plan into an Individual Retirement Account. Finally they might decide to close the 401k and receive the proceeds in cash. This would mean all money would be subject to taxes and the 10% penalty fee.

403(b) Plan

403(b) plans were created for employees of schools, churches, and tax exempt organizations. Individuals who are eligible may establish and maintain their own 403(b) accounts. Their employers can and often do make contributions to the employees' accounts. Individuals are able to open one of three different types of 403(b)s.

The first is an annuity plan that an insurance company establishes. These types of plans are sometimes called TDAs tax deferred annuities or TSAs tax sheltered annuities. A second plan type is an account which a retirement custodian offers and manages. With these 403(b)s, the account holders may only choose from mutual funds and regulated investment companies that the custodian allows. The final type is a retirement income account. These accounts accept a combination of mutual funds or annuities for the investment choices.

Employers have some control over these accounts. They are able to decide which financial institution will hold the employees' 403(b) accounts. This determines the kind of plan that the employees are able to set up and fund. Employers receive several advantages from choosing to offer a 403(b).

The benefits which they get to offer their employees are worthwhile. This helps to ensure valuable employees stay with the organization. They also enjoy sharing the funding costs between themselves and their employees. Employers may also choose for the 403(b) to only accept employee contributions if they do not wish to participate financially in the account.

Employees also experience several benefits from these types of retirement vehicles. They may contribute tax deferred dollars from their income. They may also contribute taxed dollars to the accounts. In these Roth 403(b)s, all of their earnings accrue tax free for the entire life of the account. Deferred tax payments until retirement typically allow for the employees to pay fewer taxes as they are often in a more advantageous tax bracket at retirement point. Employees may also obtain loans from their 403(b) accounts as they need them.

A variety of non profit organizations may choose to establish such a 403(b) plan for their employees. This includes any 501(c)(3) tax exempt organization, co-op hospital service organizations, public school systems, ministers at churches, Native American public school systems, and (USUHS) Uniformed Services for the University of the Health Sciences.

Such 403(b) plans can obtain a variety of contribution types. Employees may have elective deferral contributions taken out of each paycheck. These are taken out in a pretax dollars arrangement. Employees also have the ability to contribute taxed dollars to the accounts. They have these deducted from their payrolls as well.

Employers may also choose to make contributions which are either discretionary or fixed amounts as they desire. Employees and employers may make contributions to Roth 403(b) accounts. These 403(b) accounts may also receive any combination of the previously mentioned contribution types, which demonstrates their flexibility.

Employees have generous annual contribution limits with these plans. In 2016, they may contribute up to $18,000 (or $24,000 if they are over 50 years old and catching up on contributions for retirement). For 2016, employers may also deposit as much as $53,000 (up to 100% of the employee compensation) as an annual contribution.

Regarding distributions, the rules are comparable to the other types of retirement savings vehicles. Distributions of deferred taxed dollars become taxable like regular income when the employee receives them. If these are taken before the employee turns 59 ½, then the withdrawn dollars are assessed the standard 10% penalty for early withdrawals. There are some exceptions to this penalty for which an employee may qualify. One of these exceptions is if the employee terminates the job even before reaching the age of retirement.

Accountant

Accountants are professional financial personnel whose careers are centered on dealing with money and figures. Their responsibilities cover compiling financial records, certifying them, and recording them for businesses, individuals, government organizations, and not for profit organizations. As such, they track a company or individual's money through the development of reports.

Managers of companies and organizations and other individuals read these accounting reports. The managers learn the state and progress of their company from them. Governments utilize these reports to determine the taxes that companies are required to pay. Investors and other businesses look at them to determine if they wish to work with a company. Banks and others investigate these reports in their decisions of lending money to a company.

The majority of accountants are specialized. Four main types of accountants practice their trade. Management accountants follow the money that is both earned and spent by their employing companies.

Public accountants work at public accounting firms. Here, they perform auditing, accounting, consulting, and tax preparation work. These types of accountants perform numerous tasks for individuals who are clients of the accounting firm. Some public accountants have their own small business.

Government auditors and accountants ensure that the accounting records of government agencies are correct. Besides this, they double check the record of those individuals who transact business with the government. This helps to keep governments responsible.

Internal auditors are accountants who ensure that the accounting records of their company are correct. In this role, they are investigating to make certain that no person within the firm is stealing. Besides this, they investigate to make certain that no individual in the company is wasting the firm's capital.

Accountants perform their tasks in offices. Those accountants who work for public companies and government groups often travel to perform audits of their own company's other branches or outside companies. Regarding their hours, accountants typically work for a normal forty hours per week. Some accountants ply their trade for more than fifty hours each week. Especially in tax season that runs from January through April, tax accountants commonly work incredibly long hours.

The outlook for accountants is exceptionally strong. Their field of work is anticipated to grow substantially faster than the average occupation through at least 2018. The reasons for this have much to do with the complex nature of both income tax laws and mandatory financial reporting. Because of the nature of these laws and rules, the demand for accountants will always exist. Working as an accountant entails a wide variety of requirements and prerequisites. Some very important positions mandate advanced degrees. Other accountant positions only need an ability and compliance to learn the trade, along with the necessary patience to see the training through.

Adjustable Rate Mortgage (ARM)

Adjustable Rate Mortgages, also known by their acronym ARM's, are those mortgages whose interest rates change from time to time. These changes commonly occur based on an index. As a result of changing interest rates, payments will rise and fall along with them.

Adjustable Rate Mortgages involve a number of different elements. These include margins, indexes, discounts, negative amortization, caps on payments and rates, recalculating of your loan, and payment options. When considering an adjustable rate mortgage, you should always understand both the most that your monthly payments might go up, as well as your ability to make these higher payments in the future.

Initial payments and rates are important to understand with these ARM's. They stay in effect for only certain time frames that run from merely a month to as long as five years or longer. With some of these ARM's, these initial payments and rates will vary tremendously from those that are in effect later in the life of the loan. Your payments and rates can change significantly even when interest rates remain level. A way to determine how much this will vary on a particular ARM loan is to compare the annual percentage rate and the initial rate. Should this APR prove to be much greater than the initial rate, then likely the payments and rates will similarly turn out to be significantly greater when the loan adjusts.

It is important to understand that the majority of Adjustable Rate Mortgages' monthly payments and interest rates will vary by the month, the quarter, the year, the three year period, and the five year time frame. The time between these changes in rate is referred to as the adjustment period. Loans that feature one year periods are called one year ARM's, as an example.

These Adjustable Rate Mortgages' interest rates are comprised of two portions of index and margin. The index actually follows interest rates themselves. Your payments are impacted by limits on how far the rate can rise or fall. As the index rises, so will your interest rates and payments generally. As the index declines, your monthly payments could similarly fall, assuming that your ARM is one that adjusts down. ARM rates can be based on a number of different indexes, including LIBOR the London Interbank Offered rate, COFI the Cost of Funds Index, and a CMT one year constant maturity Treasury security. Other lenders use their own proprietary model.

Margin proves to be the premium to the rate that a lender itself adds. This is commonly a couple of percentage points that are added directly to the index rate amount. These amounts vary from one lender to the next, and are commonly fixed during the loan term. The fully indexed rate is comprised of index plus margin. When the loan's initial rate turns out to be lower than the fully indexed rate, this is referred to as a discounted index rate. So an index that sat at five percent and had a three percent margin tacked on would be a fully indexed rate of eight percent.

American Express

The American Express Company proves to be the New York City headquartered multinational financial services outfit. It was established in 1850 and today is among the 30 constituents of the Dow Jones Industrial Average. The company is world renowned for its various traveler's checks, chard card, and credit card businesses. The Amex cards make up around 24 percent of all credit card transaction dollar volume for the United States.

Interbrand and *Business Week* together rank American Express at number 22 for most valuable brands in the globe. They have estimated the Amex brand to be valued at almost $15 billion. *Fortune* magazine has Amex in its coveted "Top 20 Most Admired Companies in the World." Their logo is recognized around the globe. This Centurion image dates back to its unveiling in 1958. The logo is found on their credit cards, charge cards, and traveler's checks.

American Express has long served as an engine for American based commerce. Their innovative solutions cover expense management, payment needs, and travel planning for both businesses large and small and consumers. They assist their customers in achieving their goals and dreams with their benefits that lead the industry, insights into building businesses, access to one of a kind experiences, and worldwide customer care services.

When ranked by purchase volume, American Express boasts being the biggest card issuer in the world. To this effect, their company processes literally millions of individual transactions every day. They call themselves the leading network for card members who are high spenders.

Companies benefit from the many advantages that Amex offers them as well. Small businesses and their owners receive financial control and flexibility along with additional purchasing power and cash flow help. Large corporations obtain commercial payment expertise and tools to help them effectively manage their spending. This saves an aggregate of billions of dollars. Merchants are able to improve their business by utilizing Amex's information management and marketing insights.

Card members enjoy the many benefits that American Express delivers. Their travel network turns out to be among the biggest in the world. They provide a wide range of rewards programs that lead the credit card industry. The company has consistently been regarded and awarded as the industry leading company for innovation. Customers benefit from 24 hours per day, seven days per week customer service that is offered around the globe.

American Express did not begin life as a financial services company. The firm's founders Henry Wells, William Fargo, and John Warren Butterfield merged their companies to create an express mail business found in Buffalo, New York. While sister company at the time Wells Fargo & Co ran operations in California and the West, American Express handled New York state movement and shipment of goods, currencies, and securities.

They were so successful in their express shipment business that they enjoyed a New York statewide virtually monopoly of these shipments for many years. Their original entrée into financial services came when they started offering money orders in 1882 to compete with U.S. Post Office money orders. They began issuing their famed traveler's checks in 1891 in denominations including $10, $20, $50, and $100 amounts.

Amortization

The word amortization is one that is commonly utilized by financial officers of corporations and accountants. They utilize it when they are working with time concepts and how they relate to financial statements of accounts. You typically hear this word employed when you are figuring up loan calculations, or when you are determining interest payments.

The concept of amortization possesses a lengthy history and it is currently employed in numerous different segments of finance. The word itself descends from Middle English. Here amortisen meant to "alienate" or "kill" something. This derivation itself comes from the Latin admortire that signified "plus death." It is loosely related to the derivation of the word mortgage, as well.

This accounting principle is much like depreciation that diminishes a liability or asset's value over a given period of time through payments. It covers the practical life span of a tangible asset. With liabilities, it includes a pre-set amount of time over which money is paid back. Like this, a certain amount of money is set aside for the loan repayment over its lifetime.

Even though depreciation is similar to amortization, they are not the same concepts. The main difference between them lies in what they cover. While depreciation is most commonly employed to describe physical assets like property, vehicles, or buildings, amortization instead covers intangibles such as product development, copyrights, or patents. Where liabilities are concerned, it relates to income in the future that will be paid out over a given amount of time. Depreciation is instead a lost income over a time period.

Several different kinds of amortization are presently in use. This varies with the accounting method that is practiced. Business amortization deals with borrowed funds and loans and the paying of particular amounts in different time frames. When used as amortization analysis, this is the means of cost execution analysis for a given group of operations. Where tax law is concerned, amortization pertains to the interest amount that is paid over a given span of time relevant to payments and tax rates.

Amortization can also be employed with regards to zoning rules and regulations, since it conveys a property owner's time for relocating as a result of zoning guidelines and pre-existing use. Another variation is used as negative amortization. This pertains specifically to increasing loan amounts that result from total interest due not being paid up at the appropriate time.

Amortization can also be employed over a widely ranging time frame. It could cover only a year or extend to as many as forty years. This depends on the kind of loan or asset utilized. Some examples include building loans that span over as many as forty years and car loans that commonly span over merely four to five years. Asset examples would be patent right expenses that commonly are spread out over seventeen years.

Annual Percentage Rate (APR)

The annual percentage rate, or APR, is the actual interest rate that a loan charges each year. This single percentage number is truthfully used to represent the literal annual expense of using money over the life span of a given loan. Annual percentage rate not only covers interest charged, but can also be comprised of extra costs or fees that are attached to a given loan transaction.

Credit cards and loans commonly offer differing explanations for transaction fees, the structure of their interest rates, and any late fees that are assessed. The annual percentage rate provides an easy to understand formula for expressing to borrowers the real and actual percentage number of fees and interest so that they can measure these up against the rates that other possible lenders will charge them.

Annual percentage rate can include many different elements besides interest. With a nominal APR, it simply involves the rate of a given payment period multiplied out to the exact numbers of payment periods existing in a year. The effective APR is often referred to as the mathematically true rate of interest for a given year. Effective APR's are commonly the fees charged plus the rate of compound interest.

On a home mortgage, effective annual percentage rates could factor in Private Mortgage Insurance, discount points, and even processing costs. Some hidden fees do not make their ways into an effective APR number. Because of this, you should always read the fine print surrounding an APR and the costs associated with a mortgage or loan. As an example of how an effective APR can be deceptive with mortgages, the one time fees that are charged in the front of a mortgage are commonly assumed to be divided over a loan's long repayment period. If you only utilize the loan for a short time frame, then the APR number will be thrown off by this. An effective APR on a mortgage might look lower than it actually is when the loan will be paid off significantly earlier than the term of the loan.

The government created the concept of annual percentage rate to stop loan companies and credit cards issuers from deceiving consumers with fancy expressions of interest charges and fees. The law requires that all loan issuers and credit card companies have to demonstrate this annual percentage rate to all customers. This is so the consumers will obtain a fair comprehension of the true rates that are associated with their particular transactions. While credit card companies are in fact permitted to promote their monthly basis of interest rates, they still have to clearly show the actual annual percentage rate to their customers in advance of a contract or agreement being signed by the consumer.

Annual percentage rate is sometimes confused with annual percentage yield. This can be vastly different from the APR. Annual percentage yield includes calculations of compounded interest in its numbers.

Appraisal

Appraisals are professionally done estimates of a property's real value. These are conducted by appraisers. Many things can have an appraisal done on them, including smaller items like artwork or jewelry, as well as larger things like businesses, commercial buildings, or homes.

Appraisals are commonly required before many different transactions can be performed. In advance of getting a house, piece of jewelry, or an artwork insured, appraisals must be performed. Homes and offices have to be appraised for insurance, loans, and tax purposes. Appraisals ensure that these loans and insurance policies are comparable to the property's tangible market value.

Several different types of appraisals can be performed. Real property appraisal involves properly estimating Real Estate value. Personal property appraisal involves determining the worth of valuable individual objects like expensive china, jewelry, pottery, artwork, heirlooms, and antiques. Mass appraisals merge real property and personal property appraisals into a single appraisal. Business value appraisals consider all of the valuable tangible and intangible assets that a business owns, including logos, services, equipment, property, inventory, other assets and goodwill.

Perhaps the most commonly used type of appraisal is a home appraisal. Home appraisals prove to be professionally done surveys of a house to come up with an opinion or estimate of the home's value on the market. These kinds of appraisals are usually performed for banks that are considering the approval of a loan for a person purchasing a home. Such home appraisals turn out to be detailed reports. These cover many things including the home's neighborhood, the house's condition, how rapidly area houses sell, and what comparable houses actually sell for at the time.

Such a home appraisal could similarly be done for a replacement value for insurance purposes or as a sales comparison in marketing a home, as well. Cost and replacement appraisals determine what the actual cost to completely replace your home would be if something destroyed the house. This type of appraisal is most often employed for new houses. Sales comparison appraisals more often examine various additional properties within your house's neighborhood to determine at what price they are presently selling. The appraiser will then determine how such houses compare and contrast against your particular home.

Home appraisals commonly cost in the range of from $300 to $500 when people decide to order one done themselves. Such appraisals are not often accepted by banks. They will want to have their own contracted appraiser make the estimate in order to get a more independent number that they trust.

Home appraisers are always licensed by the state in which they operate. The highest of ethical standards are demanded of them. Their sole purpose is to act as an independent third party who will give their truthful opinion of a home's market value. Appraisers are not supposed to be associated with any party that is involved in the selling of a home.

Appraised Value

Appraised Value refers to the property value evaluation from a certain frozen moment in time. Professional appraisers perform these appraisals when the origination process of the mortgage is underway. Lenders themselves typically select specific property appraisers to do them. It is the borrowers who are expected to pay for getting the appraisal.

Home appraised value proves to be a critical factor in getting through the process of loan underwriting. It enjoys a special place in deciding the amount of money that buyers can borrow and according to what terms. As a key example, the LTV Loan to Value ratio is determined utilizing the appraised value. When the LTV proves to be higher than 80 percent, the lender will insist that the borrowers purchase PMI private mortgage insurance. Once the LTV declines to 78 percent or lower with an appraisal, the need for expensive PMI payments can be excused.

This appraised value should not be confused with market value. The two are both important in residential home transactions, for retail buildings, commercial property, land, and farms. Yet real distinctions between the appraised value and market value of real estate exist. The market values will be driven by consumers and their demand versus available home supply in a given city, county, or even region. The experts make the appraised values.

Appraised values of given properties relay the information in the form of a precise number on the value of the home or other property in question. These appraised values come from both the professional opinion of the appraiser as well as the data they gather from similar home sales on the same street, in the neighborhood, and in that section of the city. Market values on the other hand vary more dramatically. Buyers have great influence on the property's market value. This is because any home is ultimately truly worth as much as a buyer will actually pay for it.

Sometimes people also confuse the idea of assessed value and appraised value. Assessed values are those which the city or town assessor's office will put on a given property. They do this so that they can decide what amount of taxes should be levied and collected for the property tax. Whole towns and cities become assessed in a particular (from four months to twelve months) period. Qualified assistants will actually determine the final values once they interview the owners and examine the properties in question. Municipalities then combine all of the assessed values for all properties within their jurisdiction to determine how much the tax rate should be for the year in question. It is possible for the town or city to revalue its tax rate every year in order to gather the revenues they require to run the municipality. This means that while assessments do not typically change on a yearly basis, tax rates could.

It is only in cases where the city or town's assessed values are deemed to be outdated that they will reassess the properties in the jurisdiction. This happens as dramatic inequities arise between one property and the next. It would require a sufficient reason to spend the money on conducting a new assessment of all properties within the municipality. There are states which have standard regulations that each home must be reassessed on an individual basis whenever it becomes sold or transferred. It is also true that rarely will the assessed values versus the appraised values for a given property be precisely the same dollar amount. This is because while assessed values are not impacted by market activity in a certain time period, the appraised values will inevitably be influenced by them due to actual market activity of homes selling in the area.

Assets

Assets are any thing that can be owned by a company or an individual person. These are able to be sold for cash. Commonly, assets produce income or give value to the owner.

In the world of financial accounting, assets prove to be economic resources. They can be physical objects or intangible concepts that can be utilized and owned to create value. Assets are deemed to have real and positive value for their owners. Assets must also be convertible into cash, which itself is furthermore considered to be an asset.

There are several different types of assets as measured by accountants and accounting processes. These might be current assets, longer term assets, intangible assets, or deferred assets. Current assets include cash and other items that are readily and easily able to be sold to raise cash. Longer term assets are those that are held and useful for great periods of time, including such physical items as factory plants, real estate, and equipment. Intangible assets are non physical rights or concepts, like patents, trademarks, goodwill, and copyrights. Finally, deferred assets are those that involve monies spent now for the costs in the future of things like rent, insurance, or interest.

Though tangible, physical assets are not hard to conceptualize, intangible assets are often confusing for people to understand. Even though these are not physical items that may be touched, they still have value that can be controlled and sold to raise cash. Intangible assets include rights and resources which provide a company with a form of marketplace advantage. These can cover many different elements beyond those listed above, such as computer programs, stocks, bonds, and even accounts receivable.

On balance sheets, tangible assets are commonly divided into further categories. These include fixed assets and current assets. Fixed assets are objects that are immobile or not easily transported, such as buildings, office locations, and equipment. Current assets are comprised of inventory that a business holds. Balance sheets of companies keep track of a firm's assets and their value as expressed in monetary terms. These assets are both the cash and other items that the business or person owns.

Assets should never be confused with liabilities. Assets create positive cash flow that represents value or money coming into a business, organization, or individual's accounts. Liabilities are obligations that have to be paid and that create negative cash flow, or take money out of a business, individual, or organization's accounts. As an example of the difference between the two, assets would be houses that are rented out that bring in more rent every month than the expenses, interest, and upkeep of the houses. Liabilities would be homes that have payments that must be paid every month and do not provide any income stream to effectively offset this.

Bad Debt

Bad debts are those accounts receivable that simply can not be collected. Once businesses make the determination that they are not likely to be able to collect on such sums, then they actually write these off as complete losses for the company. A debt is not typically deemed to be un-collectable until every effort within reason has been made to collect on the debt that is owed. This status is not typically reached on a debt until the person or firm owing the debt has filed for bankruptcy. Another reason for a debt to be declared a bad debt would be when the costs of continuing to collect on the debt are greater than is the amount of the debt in question.

Such bad debts commonly show up on a company income statement as an expense. This actually reduces the company's net income. At this point, bad debts have been completely written off via crediting the account of the debtor. This cancels out any remaining balance on the debtor's account. Such bad debts prove to be money that has been totally lost by a firm. Because of this, these kinds of bad debts are referred to as expenses for a business.

Companies attempt to estimate their expenses in the form of bad debts using records from similar past time frames. They look to figure out how many bad debts will show up in the current time frame based on what happened before so that they can attempt to estimate their actual earnings. The majority of corporations come up with an allowance for bad debts, as they understand that a percentage of their debtors will never repay them completely. Banks and credit card companies are especially concerned with bad debt allowances, since much of their entire business model revolves around the issuing of credit and repayment of debts from businesses and individuals.

The real difficulty with bad debts lies in determining if and when they are actually dead. When a debtor disappears, the collateral is destroyed, a lawsuit statute of limitations expires, bankruptcy is discharged, or significant pattern of a debtor abandoning debts is present, then a debt is finally determined to be bad debt. These can be subjective measurements in some cases.

Income tax laws contain a different definition for bad debts. These debts can be deducted against regular income on a 1040 C Form. These personal debts are also able to be deducted against short term types of capital gains. Debts that are owed for services which have been rendered to a person or business are not considered taxing purpose bad debts. This is because no income is present for such unpaid services that can be taxed.

Where individuals are concerned, bad debt can refer to credit card debt or any other form of high interest debt. These kinds of debts take away money from the individual in interest payments every month, creating a negative cash flow. Good debt for an individual would be debt that is used to properly leverage investments. Such leveraged investments that create positive cash flow prove to be the most desirable forms of debt.

Bankruptcy

Bankruptcy is a term that refers to the elimination or restructuring of a person or company's debt. Three principal different types of bankruptcy filing are available. These are the personal bankruptcy options of Chapter 7 and Chapter 13 filings, and the business bankruptcy restructuring option of Chapter 11.

Individuals avail themselves of Chapter 7 or Chapter 13 bankruptcy filings when their financial situations warrant significant help. With a Chapter 7 filing, all of an individual's debt is erased through discharge. This provides a new start for the debtor. Due to changes in laws made back in October 2005, not every person is able to obtain this type of total debt relief any longer. As a result of this new bankruptcy law, a means test came into being that prospective bankruptcy filers must successfully pass if they are to prove eligibility for this kind of bankruptcy relief.

The net effect of this new test is that consumers find it much more difficult to qualify for total debt elimination under Chapter 7. Besides the means test, the cost of bankruptcy attorneys has now risen dramatically by upwards of a hundred percent as a result of the new laws. Before these laws went into effect, Chapter 7 filings represented around seventy percent of all personal filings for bankruptcy. Chapter 7 offered the individual the advantage of simply walking away from debts that they might be capable of paying back with sufficient time and some interest rate help.

Chapter 13 Bankruptcy filings prove to be much like debt restructuring procedures. In these proceedings, a person's creditors are made to agree to the repayment of principal and zero interest on debts over a longer span of time. The individual gets to keep all of her or his assets in this form of filing. The most common motivation for Chapter 13 proves to be a desire to stop a foreclosure on a home. Individuals are able to achieve this by halting foreclosure proceedings and catch up on back mortgage payments. Once a court examines the debtor's budget, it will sign off on the plan for repayment proposed by the person. Depending on the level of an individual's income, he or she may have no choice but to file a Chapter 13 filling, as a result to the 2005 law changes.

Companies and corporations that are in financial distress may avail themselves of bankruptcy protection as well. Chapter 11 allows for such businesses to have protection from their creditors while they restructure their debt. Some individuals who have a higher income level will take advantage of this form of filing as well, since it does not place income restrictions on the entity filing. It has been instrumental in saving many large and well known companies over the years, including K-Mart, that actually emerged strong enough from the Chapter 11 bankruptcy to buy out higher end rival Sears afterward.

Bitcoin Currency (BTC)

Bitcoin is the name of a new electronic currency. An unknown individual who called himself Satoshi Nakamoto created this currency in 2009. This world's first widespread virtual currency appeals to many individuals because there are no banks or governments involved in issuing, trading, spending, or processing the transactions. There are also no transaction fees involved. Owners do not have to provide their actual identity to use them.

Bitcoin users like that they are able to purchase goods and services completely anonymously. They also enjoy the inexpensive and simple to use international payment system. This exists because this currency is not heavily regulated nor tied to any single bank or nation. Small businesses tend to like Bitcoin since they do not have to pay any credit card usage fees.

Many speculators have purchased Bitcoins for investment. Booms and busts in this currency are all too common. Those who bought in to the crypto currency early made spectacular returns as the value skyrocketed with growing demand. Others lost fortunes as the price of the Bitcoins subsequently crashed in value.

There are several ways to obtain these Bitcoins. Users buy them on open marketplaces known as Bitcoin exchanges. Those who wish to have them can buy and sell it with a variety of different currencies. Mt. Gox was the largest Bitcoin marketplace until it spectacularly collapsed and went bankrupt. Many clients who held their Bitcoins at Mt. Gox lost most of their money there at the time.

Individuals also buy and sell Bitcoins by transferring them to each other and by paying with them. They can do this with their computers or mobile apps. This is much like sending cash with a digital service like PayPal.

A last way to obtain Bitcoins is by mining them. Mining is the way that individuals create new Bitcoins. They do this by utilizing computers to solve complicated math problems or puzzles. When such a puzzle is solved, 25 Bitcoins are awarded to the group which solves them.

Owners keep their Bitcoins in a digital wallet. This can be stored on a personal computer or in the cloud. A virtual wallet is much like an electronic bank account which permits owners to receive or send Bitcoins, to save their money, or to pay for their goods and services. These wallets do not receive the protection of FDIC insurance as do traditional bank accounts.

To users, Bitcoins are simply computer programs or mobile apps which give the owners the Bitcoin wallet. The payment system is easier to utilize than is a credit card or debit card purchase. An individual does not require a merchant account in order to receive the currency. All an individual has to do to make a payment is to put the payment amount and address of the recipient then click send.

An important fact about Bitcoin is that no one owns the actual network. Bitcoin users control the Bitcoin currency. Various developers work on the software to improve it. Users are able to decide which version or software they use it on, which prohibits developers from forcefully changing the operation. For the software to work properly, all Bitcoin users have to work with programs that abide by the same rules.

As with most new currencies Bitcoin is not without problems. When digital wallets are left in the cloud, some servers have been hacked and coins stolen. Bitcoin exchanges like Mt. Gox have failed. Other companies have disappeared with their clients' Bitcoins. When the wallets stay on a person's computer, they can be destroyed by viruses or accidentally deleted.

Increasing government regulation appears to be in the future of Bitcoin and other crypto currencies. Because of the anonymous nature of the currency, they have evolved into the preferred payment method for illegal activities such as drugs and smuggling. Governments are concerned about being able to trace these types of activities back to the users. They are also worried about not being able to tax transactions made in Bitcoin currency.

Blockchain

Blockchain refers to a technology that serves as a means of structuring and storing data. As such it is the ultimate foundation of the revolutionary cryptocurrencies such as Bitcoin and Ether. The true breakthrough in coding capability permits participants to share digital ledgers back and forth over a computer network. Its genius and appeal lies in the fact that it does not require a central authority to run or oversee it. Since there is no meddling central authority like a central bank or boss to the system, no one party can interfere with the financial records.

In other words, the straight math makes sure that all the parties who participate are honest with each other. Blockchain is made up of concatenated transactions blocks. Nowadays, the technology has become so important and offers so many future possibilities for real world applications that over forty of the world's biggest and most important financial firms are experimenting with uses for it.

Blockchains are also public record ledgers of all transactions in a cryptocurrency which have ever taken place. For this reason, the chain is always expanding as every new record adds additional completed blocks to it. These become a part of the blockchain via a chronological and linear fashioned order. Every participating node receives a copy of this blockchain as it is updated. Nodes are computers which share a Bitcoin network connection that utilizes the system to validate and relay such transactions which were performed in it. The chain comes as an auto download once a computer network joins up to the Bitcoin network. This chain maintains full information on all balances and appropriate addresses from the very first transaction ever all the way to the latest one which has been performed utilizing the block.

In the end, it is this blockchain that represents the primary technological advance offered by Bitcoin. It amounts to the proof and record of every transaction performed using the network. The blocks represent the current record in the chain that will ultimately record all or at least some of the recent transaction. After it is finished, this block will join the chain as part and parcel of the current and permanent database. Once a block is spoken for, a new block will become generated. Myriads of such blocks exist in the chain. They are linked one to another, much like a physical chain, in their correct chronological and linear order. Each block contains the hash of the prior block in it.

It is always helpful to consider a real world example to better understand a somewhat complex concept like this one. Traditional banking is a solid analogy. This blockchain is much like a complete history of banking records and transactions. Bitcoin transactions must be chronologically entered in the blockchain as real world banking transactions are at financial institutions. Such blocks are something like the statements recording individual bank accounts and banking transactions.

The protocol of Bitcoin is based upon all nodes in the system sharing the blockchain's database. A complete and unaltered copy of the chain will include records of all the transactions in Bitcoin which have ever been executed. This delivers useful insights into the quantity of value that a specific address owned at any time in the past.

The problem with the ever growing nature of the chain is that it has become so very large with over a decade of increasing size that synchronization and storage have become serious issues. These days, the average time of a new block appearing on the chain amounts to only ten minutes. Mining, the process of unlocking new BTC, is adding the majority of new blocks to the chain these days.

Bonds

Bonds are also known as debt instruments, fixed income securities, and credit securities. A bond is actually an IOU contract where the terms of the bond, interest rate, and date of repayment are all particularly defined in a legal document. If you buy a bond at original issue, then you are literally loaning the issuer money that will be repaid to you at a certain time, along with periodic interest payments.

Bonds are all classified under one of three categories in the United States. The first of these are the highest rated, safest category of Federal Government debt and its associated agencies. Treasury bills and treasury bonds fall under this first category. The second types of bonds are bonds deemed to be safe that are issued by companies, states, and cities. These first two categories of bonds are referred to as investment grade. The third category of bonds involves riskier types of bonds that are offered by companies, states, and cities. Such below investment grade bonds are commonly referred to as simply junk bonds.

Bonds' values rise and fall in directly opposite correlation to the movement of interest rates. As interest rates fall, bonds rise. When interest rates are rising, bonds prices fall. These swings up and down in interest rates and bond prices are not important to you if you buy a bond and hold it until the pay back, or maturity, date. If you choose to sell a bond before maturity, the price that it realizes will be mostly dependent on what the interest rates prove to be like at the time.

Bonds' investment statuses are rated by the credit rating agencies. These are Standard & Poor's, Moody's, and Fitch Ratings. All bond debt issues are awarded easy to understand grades, such as A+ or B. In the last few years of the financial crisis, these credit rating agencies were reprimanded for having awarded some companies bonds' too high grades considering the risks that the companies undertook. This was especially the case with the bonds of banks, investment companies, and some insurance outfits.

Understanding the bond markets is a function of comprehending the yield curves. Yield curves turn out to be pictorial representations of a bond's interest rate and the date that it reaches maturity, rendered on a graph.

Learning to understand and read these curves, and to figure out the spread between such curves, will allow you to make educated comparisons between various issues of bonds.

Some bonds are tax free. These are those bonds that are offered by states and cities. Such municipal bonds, also known as munis, help to raise funds that are utilized to pay for roads, schools, dams, and various other projects. Interest payments made on these municipal bonds are not subject to Federal taxes. This makes them attractive to some investors.

Brexit

Brexit refers to the Jun 23, 2016 referendum on the future of Britain in the European Union. The term comes from the Grexit reference to the potential for Greece to leave the Eurozone shared currency area in past years. In this historic referendum, British voters have to answer the question "Should the UK remain a member of the EU or leave the EU?" Britain's electoral commission came up with the phrasing of the question and parliament accepted it.

The question of having a referendum on the issue arose in the 2015 general election in the U.K. Prime Minister David Cameron promised voters that he would offer the British people a final say on the issue of remaining in the EU if he won reelection. His ruling conservative party has been split on the Euro-skeptic idea and EU membership for around 40 years. The individual on the ground Conservative members are largely for exiting from the European Union over a variety of issues of sovereignty and border and legal control.

Those in favor of Britain leaving the EU believe that the restrictive rules hamper creation of new jobs. They also want to be able to decide on which laws to pass and on their trading partners. Though parliament in London passes laws, these can and have been overturned by the European Parliament and courts in Brussels.

Part of the reason the government decided to hold the referendum in early summer was to have it over before the next summer migration crisis begins in earnest. This migration problem has recently stirred up anger and fear in British citizens that they are losing control of their migration policy to the European Union in Brussels. Proponents of the leave campaign want to make their own immigration policy and decide on who comes into the country.

Those in favor of staying in the EU have their own reasons for their position. They feel that remaining in the block of European countries increases the nation's economic, military, and global influence around the world. Remain campaigners argue that Britain is stronger and more secure at home and abroad by being a part of this largest economic block in the world.

The voting base for this historic referendum is different than for general elections. Any British citizen who is older than 18 is allowed to vote. Citizens of the Commonwealth of Nations who reside in Britain are also eligible to cast ballots. There are 53 member nations of the Commonwealth. This means that residents in Britain of such countries and entities as Canada, Australia, New Zealand, Ireland, Malta, Cyprus, and Gibraltar will be allowed to vote on the Brexit issue.

Brexit supports have argued that the European Union has many incentives to continue trading with the United Kingdom. It remains a large importer of services and goods and carries out much of its trade with the block. They feel that they will be able to forge new and better trade agreements with the rest of the world. This would save them more than 8 billion pounds in contributions made to the European Union budget every year. They believe that the country will be able to join Norway, Iceland, and Liechtenstein as a European Economic Area member nation.

Those who favor remaining in the EU argue that leaving the block will create too much uncertainty in British markets. They argue that foreign companies will not be so likely to invest in Britain and others may move their EU regional or international headquarters to other countries should Britain cease to have unfettered access to the common market.

The Treasury has predicted that a recession created by leaving the EU block would cost households 4,300 Pounds per year in lost jobs, trade, and higher taxes by the year 2030. They argue that the pound will weaken substantially and push up the costs for weekly shopping, travel, and imported goods. Others are worried about what will happen to outside Europeans living in Britain and British expatriates who live around Europe after an exit from the European Union.

Brokers

Brokers are professional intermediaries that work on behalf of both a seller and a buyer. When brokers function as agents on behalf of only a buyer or seller, they become representatives and principal parties in any deal. Brokers should not be confused with agents, who instead work on the behalf of a single principal. In the financial world, there are stock brokers, commodity brokers, and option brokers.

Stock brokers are highly regulated broker professionals that sell and buy stock shares and related securities. They work on the part of investors who purchase and sell such securities. Stock brokers transact through either Agency Only Firms or market makers in a given security. These types of brokers are commonly employees of brokerage firms, such as Morgan Stanley, Prudential, or UBS.

Stock brokers are essential in stock transactions, since these exchanges of stocks can only occur between two individuals who are actual members of the exchange in question. A regular investor can not simply enter a stock exchange like the NASDAQ and ask to buy or sell a stock. This is the role that brokers fulfill.

Within the stock broker realm, three different kinds of broker services exist. One of these is advisory dealing, in which a broker makes recommendations to the client of what types of shares to purchase and sell, yet allows the investor to enact the ultimate decision. A second type is an execution only broker, who will simply transact the customer's specific buying and selling instructions. Finally, discretionary dealing involves brokers who learn all about the customer's goals in investing then carry out trades for the customer based on his or her interests.

These same functions are carried out by other financial market brokers as well. Commodities brokers deal in commodities contracts for clients in commodities such as gold, silver, wheat, and oil. Commodities contracts are comprised of options, futures, and financial derivatives. These commodities brokers act as middle men to an investor to transact buy and sell orders on such commodities exchanges as the New York Mercantile Exchange, Commodities Mercantile Exchange, and New York Board of

Trade.

Options brokers deal in options on stocks, commodities, or currencies, depending on what their area of specialty proves to be. They specialize in providing research, trading, and education on options to individual investor clients. Besides handling the main options that include straddles, option spreads, and covered calls, a number of options brokers facilitate trade in related fields that include ETF's, stocks, bonds, and mutual funds.

Brokers in the financial world are typically regulated by one oversight group or another. Stock brokers, for example, are licensed and overseen by the Securities Exchange Commission. They must pass an exam called the Series 7 in order to practice their trade as a stock broker. Commodities brokers, on the other hand, must obtain a Series 3 license from the Financial Industry Regulatory Authority. They are closely monitored by the Commodities Futures Trading Commission. Options brokers are monitored by the regulatory agency associated with the area of options that they trade.

Bull Market

A bull market is one in which an entire financial market or a select grouping of securities sees rising prices over an extended period of time. It is also used to describe a scenario in which prices are expected to rise. While the phrase bull market is most frequently utilized to address the stock markets, it can similarly reference any items that trade, such as sustained rising prices in commodities, currencies, or bonds. The opposite of a bull market is a bear market.

The simplest definition of a bull market is one that is rising. Bull markets are those that witness an increase in prices of market shares that is sustained for a period of time. In bull markets, investors show great confidence that this rising trend will only continue to exist over a longer term. When bull markets are in effect, a nation's economy remains strong and employment levels prove to be higher.

Bull markets show the characteristics of high investor confidence, general enthusiasm about the future, and anticipation that strong and successful results will continue to occur. Forecasting with any certainty when such bull market trends will wane is challenging. Much of the problem lies in attempting to decipher speculation's role and the psychological impacts of investors that can often have a major influence on the markets in general.

Bull markets in stocks commonly develop as an economic slow down is waning. They begin in advance of an economy demonstrating a convincing recovery. As investors' confidence levels grow, they show this by their buying and investing in a belief that stock prices will gain in the future. Bull markets generally turn out to be positive and winning scenarios for most investors.

The phrase bull market is derived from the animal world, as is its opposite concept of bear markets. Bulls attack their prey by using their horns in an upward thrust, as when markets are moving up. Bears on the other hand swipe their victims down with their paws, as when markets are falling down. When the trend is rising, the market is a bull market. When it is falling instead, it is called a bear market.

Examples of bull markets abound in both the United States and developing countries. Throughout most of the 1980's and 1990's, the U.S. stock markets rose in a long running bull market. Prices rose by nearly ten fold in that time period. The Dot Com bubble put an end to this bull market at the turn of the century.

Around the world, there have also been numerous bull markets in foreign stock exchanges. In India, the Bombay Stock Exchange, known as SENSEX, experienced a dramatic bull market for five years from mid 2003 to the first of 2008. In this time frame, the index ran from 2,900 points on up to 21,000 points.

Cash Flow

Cash Flow is either an incoming revenue or outgoing expense stream that affects the value of any cash account over time. Inflows of cash, or positive cash flows, typically result from one of three possible activities, including operations, investing, or financing for businesses or individuals. Individuals are also able to realize positive cash flows from gifts or donations.

Negative cash flow is also called cash outflows. Outflows of cash happen because of either expenses or investments made. This is the case for both individuals' finances, as well as for those of businesses.

Where both individual finances and business corporate finances are concerned, positive cash flows are required to maintain solvency. Cash flows could be demonstrated because of a past transaction like selling a business product or a personal item or investment. They might also be projected into a future time for some consideration that a company or individual anticipates receiving and then possibly spending. No person or corporation can survive for long without cash flow.

Positive cash flow is essential for a variety of needs. Sufficient cash flow allows for money for you to pay your personal bills and creditors. It also allows a business to cover the costs of employee payroll, suppliers' bills, and creditors' payments in a timely fashion. When individuals and businesses lack sufficient cash on hand to maintain their budget or operations, then they are named insolvent. Lasting insolvency generally leads to personal or corporate bankruptcy.

For businesses, statements of cash flows are created by accountants. These demonstrate the quantity of cash that is created and utilized by a corporation in a certain time frame. Cash flows in this definition are calculated by totaling net income following taxes with non cash charges like depreciation. Cash flow is able to be assigned to either a business' entire operations or to one particular segment or project of the company. Cash flow is often considered to be an effective measurement of a business' ongoing financial strength.

Cash flows are also used by business and individuals to ascertain the value or return of a project or investment. The numbers of cash flows in to and out of such projects and investments are often utilized as inputs for indicators of performance like net present value and internal rate of return. A problem with a business' liquidity can also be determined by measuring the entire entity's cash flow.

Many individuals prefer investments that yield periodic positive cash flow over ones that pay only one time capital gains. High yielding dividend stocks, energy trusts, and real estate investment trusts are all examples of positive cash flow investments. Real estate properties can also be positive cash flow yielding investments when they provide greater amounts of rental income than their combined monthly mortgage payments, maintenance expenses, and property management upkeep costs and outflows total.

Cash Flow Quadrant

The cash flow quadrant is a diagram that shows four types of individuals involved in a business. These four people make up the entire business world. The four quadrants are E, S, B, and I.

The E quadrant stands for employees. Employees have the same core values in general. This is security. When any employee sits down with a manager or a president, they will always tell them the same thing. This is that they are looking for a secure and safe job that includes benefits.

The S in the cash flow quadrant represents a small business owner or a self employed person. They are generally solo actors or one person outfits. These types would rather operate on their own, as their motto is always to have something done right, you should do it yourself.

On the right side of the cash flow quadrant are the B's. B stands for Big Business people. Big businesses have five hundred or greater numbers of employees. They are completely different from the others in the quadrants, as they are constantly looking for the most intelligent and capable people, networks, and systems to aid them in running their large business. They do not want to micro manage the company themselves, rather they want good people to do it on their behalf.

The last quarter of the cash flow quadrants is the I, which stands for Investor. Investors are those individuals who make money work effectively and efficiently for themselves. The main difference between them and the B quadrants it that the investors have their money working hard while the Big Business people have other people working hard for them. Both groups of B's and I's represent the wealthy. The employees and the self employed are the people who work hard for the business people and investors on the right, or wealthy side of the quadrant.

The cash flow quadrant explains the differences between the rich and the working poor. It is useful to describe four types of income that a person can generate as well. The smartest people in the cash flow quadrant are the ones who manage to make the other people and their money work hard for their benefit. That is why they are the wealthy, while the hard working members of society on the left side are the ones who do all of the working on the wealthy people's behalf. Learning to become wealthy means effectively changing which square of the cash flow quadrant a person occupies.

Cash Savings Account

A cash savings account is a place that you can park your cash and gain interest on it. Effective short term savings accounts are ones that permit you to meet your needs in four important areas. The access to the funds is critical.

Cash savings accounts should allow you to withdraw funds from the account whenever you need. This should be accomplished through convenient methods like ATM cards or online means. Funds in all types of cash savings accounts are insured by the FDIC, or Federal Deposit Insurance Corporation, to $100,000 for all people and $250,000 for retiree accounts.

Interest is another area of concern for cash savings accounts. This pertains to the rate that the bank or institution will give you for holding your money. Larger amounts generally attract superior rates.

Penalties should not have to be endured for withdrawing cash from cash savings accounts either. Certificates of Deposits and other instruments feature such penalties, but cash savings accounts should not. These terms of withdrawal should be clearly specified in any cash savings account.

Finally, service is an issue to be considered with cash savings accounts. You might wish to have customer service in a bank branch included. Otherwise, do it yourself online accounts can be established.

There are several types of cash savings accounts from which you can choose. One is a checking account that includes interest. This might be called a money market account. Such money market accounts include check writing privileges and check based access to funds. These can be held at banks or brokerage houses, which are gaining in popularity at banks' expense. Some privileges besides check writing include higher money market rates of interest and ATM card and machine access to funds. Downsides to these types of accounts include sometimes high minimum balances and possible fees.

Standard savings accounts are another option with cash savings accounts.

These were once called passbook accounts. The interest rates provided by these accounts are lower than inflation, which proves to be their major downside. Their major advantage lies in the extremely low account minimums and fees charged to have them.

High yield bank accounts are a third type of cash savings accounts. Providing versatility of adding or withdrawing funds without penalties, they also offer the liquidity of not tying up your money for long periods of time. Nowadays, there are high yield bank accounts that provide interest rates that prove to be comparable to Certificates of Deposits, without showcasing these investments' restrictions on taking out money. The highest rates available on high yield bank accounts come from banks that are online only versions of the traditional lending institutions.

They accomplish this by not offering branches and in person customer service benefits. This means that unless such an online high yield account includes an ATM card, the only way to withdraw the funds is through electronic transfers to other brokerage, savings, or checking accounts, which can result in delays of as much as two to five full days. Without such an ATM card, it can be inconvenient to access cash stored in these accounts in a hurry or emergency situation. High yield accounts sometimes offer shorter term teaser interest rates, so individuals should investigate the product's prior six month history of interest rates to learn what their consistent rates turn out to be.

Chapter 7 Bankruptcy

Chapter 7 bankruptcy is a form of protection from creditors. Unlike Chapter 13 bankruptcy, it does not have any repayment plan. In the Chapter 7 a bankruptcy trustee determines what eligible assets the debtor individual or company has. The trustee then collects these available assets, sells them, and distributes proceeds to the creditors against their debts. This is all done under the rules of the Bankruptcy Code.

Debtors are permitted to keep specific property that is exempt, such as their house. Other property that the debtor holds will be mortgaged or have liens put against it to pledge it to the various creditors until it is liquidated. Debtors who file chapter 7 will likely forfeit property in partial payment of debts.

Chapter 7 bankruptcy is available to corporations, partnerships, and individuals who pass a means test. The relief can be granted whether or not the debtor is ruled to be insolvent.

Chapter 7 bankruptcy cases start when debtors file their petitions with their particular area's bankruptcy court. For businesses, they use the address where the main office is located. Debtors are required to give the court information that includes schedules of current expenditures and income and liabilities and assets.

They are also required to furnish a financial affairs statement and a schedule of contracts and leases which are not expired. The debtors will also have to deliver the trustee tax return copies from the most current tax year along with any tax returns which they file while the case is ongoing.

Debtors who are individuals also have to furnish their court with other documents. They are required to file a credit counseling certificate and any repayment plan created there. They must also file proof of income from employers 60 days before their original filing, a monthly income statement along with expected increases in either, and notice of interest they have in tuition or state education accounts. Husbands and wives are allowed to file individually or jointly. They must abide by the requirements for individual debtors either way.

The courts are required to charge debtors who file $335 in filing, administrative, and trustee fees. Debtors typically pay these when they file to the clerk of court. The court can give permission for individuals to pay by installments instead. When the income of debtor's proves to be less than 150% of the amount of the poverty level, the court can choose to drop the fee requirements.

Debtors will have to provide a great amount of information in order to complete their Chapter 7 filing and receive a discharge of debts. They have to list out each of their creditors along with the amounts they owe then and the type of claim. Debtors have to furnish a list of all property the own. They must also give the information on the amount, source, and frequency of income they have to the court.

Finally, they will be required to provide an in depth list of all monthly living expenses that includes housing, utilities, food, transportation, clothing, medicine, and taxes. This helps the court to determine if the debtor is able to set up a repayment plan instead of discharging the debts.

From 21 to 40 days after the debtor files the petition with the courts, the trustee hosts a creditors' meeting. The debtor will have to cooperate with the trustee on any requests for additional financial documents or records. At this meeting, the trustee will ask questions to make sure the debtor is fully aware of the consequences of debt discharge by the bankruptcy court. Sometimes trustees will deliver this in written form to the debtor before or at the meeting. Assuming the trustee makes the recommendation for discharge, the Federal bankruptcy court judge will discharge the debts when the process is completed.

Closing Costs

Closing costs are the fees that are charged when you buy a house. Many other costs are associated with buying a house than only the down payment. These closing costs are fees like recording fees, title policies, courier charges, inspections, lender fees, and start up reserve fees to create an impound account.

The most expensive component of these closing costs is the lender charged fees. Such closing costs are charged beyond the home's purchase price. Most closing costs are set and predetermined, meaning that they are not open to negotiation.

The total price of closing costs is fairly standard. Typically, a good guideline for closing costs is that they will run you somewhere between two and four percent of a house's purchase price. The range is as large as this spread because the origination fees and points for making the loan vary significantly from one lender to the next. These points and origination fees that are charged by the lender are always revealed to a buyer in the Good Faith Estimates that are provided to the buyers. For example, a home that is $400,000 will have closing costs that run from around $4,000 to $16,000. They could be even higher than this amount, on some occasions.

Some closing costs are of the non-recurring kind. Such fees are charged to a buyer of a house on only a single time. They include escrow or closing, title policies, courier fees, wire fees, notary charges, endorsements, attorney costs, city or county or state transfer taxes, recording, natural hazard disclosures, home protection plans, lender fees for the HUD-1 800 line, and home inspections.

Other closing costs are called prepaid closing costs, or recurring closing costs. Although these are paid for in a single lump sump up front, they cover those costs that continue to recur throughout the life of the home loan. There are comprised of property taxes, flood insurance when required, fire insurance premiums, prepaid interest, and private or mutual mortgage insurance premiums.

Closing costs are also impacted by the month of the year in which you close on the house in question. This is because future insurance and tax payments will be collected on a pro rated basis for the number of months of premiums for the year. Not all loans come with an escrow or impound account either. Yet loans that are for in excess of eighty percent of the purchase price of your house will mandate such an escrow account and impound be established.

Closing costs are some of the unfortunately high expenses associated with buying a house. They are only avoidable when a person takes over an assumable mortgage. In these cases, most closing costs, such as lender points and origination fees, are side stepped by a buyer.

Collateral

Collateral refers to an asset or piece of Real Estate which borrowers provide as security to lenders in exchange for a loan. This property actually secures the mortgage or other form of loan. In the event that the borrowers do not continue to make the agreed upon payments on the loan according to the laid out schedule, the financial institution has the right to seize this property in order to recover the principal losses.

Because such collateral provides at least nominal security to the lending institution in the scenarios where the borrower refuses to or is unable repay the loan, these forms of loans are commonly provided with lower interest rates as compared to those loans which are unsecured entirely. When such a lender has interest in the underlying property provided by the borrower then this is referred to as a lien.

In the end there are several arrangements with such collateral. The type of loan often determines which form will be required within the contract. With car loans or mortgages, the loans are secured by the property upon which the financial institution issues the loan. Other forms of loans have more flexible security, as with collateralized personal loans. In order for any loan to be called secured, the backing security has to be at least equal to or greater than the balance that remains on the loan in question.

Such secured loans entail far less risk for lenders because the underlying property serves as an incentive for the borrower to keep paying back the loan. Borrowers know all too well that if they do not complete the required payments then the financial institution which holds the loan may legally possess (or repossess) this collateral in order to recoup the money it is owed on the rest of the loan.

With mortgages, the collateral in question will always be the home that the borrower buys using the loan in the first place. If and when they fail to pay the debts, then the lender may seize possession of the property by utilizing a procedure called foreclosure. After the lender completes the necessary court process and has the property back in its possession, it is allowed to sell off the home to someone else. This will permit the bank to cover the principal which remains on the original loan along with their costs for the foreclosure.

Houses also can also be utilized for second mortgage collateral, or against HELOC's (Home Equity Lines of Credit). In such scenarios, the credit delivered by the financial institution may not be greater than the equity which exists within the home itself. As a tangible example, a home could have a market value of $300,000. At the same time, it might be that $175,000 of the original mortgage balance remains to pay. This would mean that the majority of HELOC's or even second mortgages would not exceed the available equity of $125,000.

Collateral is also utilized in margin accounts' trading of stocks, commodities, and futures. In this case, it is the securities themselves that become the property which secures the brokerage loan. In the event that a margin call has to be issued and the account holder will not or can not pay it on demand, then the securities' value ultimately makes certain that the brokerage will get back its loaned money.

Sometimes financial institutions will require additional collateral be put up for a given existing loan, if the contract allows such a scenario. This will reduce increasing risks for the lending institution. A creditor could give notice that without such additional security, they will be forced to raise the interest rate on the loan. Additionally accepted security could be certificates of deposit, cash, equipment, letters of credit, or even shares of stock.

Commodities

Commodities turn out to be items that are taken from the earth, such as orange juice, cattle, wheat, oil, and gold. Companies buy commodities to turn them into usable products like bread, gasoline, and jewelry to sell to other businesses and consumers. Individual investors purchase and sell them for the purposes of speculation, in an attempt to make a profit.

Commodities are traded through commodities brokers on one of several different commodities exchanges, such as COMEX, or the Commodities Mercantile Exchange, NYMEX, or the New York Mercantile Exchange, and NYBOT, or the New York Board of Trade, among others.

Commodities are traded with contracts using a great amount of leverage. This means that with a small amount of money, a great quantity of the commodity in question can be controlled and traded. For example, with only a few thousand dollars, you as an investor are able to control a contract of one thousand barrels of heating oil or one hundred ounces of gold.

As a result of this high leverage that you obtain, the amounts of money made or lost can be significant with only relatively small moves in the price of the underlying commodity. This leverage results from the fact that commodities are nearly always traded using margin accounts that lead to significant risks for the capital invested. For example, with gold contracts, each ten cent minimum price move represents a $10 per contract gain or loss.

Commodity trading strategies center around speculation on factors that will affect the production of a commodity. These could be related to weather, natural disasters, strikes, or other events. If you believed that severe hurricanes would damage a great portion of the Latin American coffee crop, then you would call your commodity broker and instruct them to buy as many coffee contracts as they had money in the account to cover.

If the hurricanes took place and coffee did see significant damage in the region, then the prices of coffee would rise dramatically as a result of the negative weather, causing the coffee harvest to be more valuable. Your coffee contracts would similarly rise in value, probably significantly.

A variety of commodities can be traded on the commodities exchanges. These include grains, metals, energy, livestock, and softs. Grains consistently prove to be among the most popular of commodities available to trade. Grain commodities are usually most active in the spring and summer. Grains include soybeans, corn, oats, wheat, and rough rice.

Metals commodities offer you the opportunity to take positions on precious metals such as gold and silver. Changes in the underlying prices of base metals may also be traded in this category. Metals include copper, silver, and gold.

Energy commodities that you can trade are those used for heating homes and fueling vehicles for the nation. With the energy complex you can trade on supply disruptions around the world or higher gas prices that you anticipate. Energy commodities available to you are crude oil, unleaded gas, heating oil, and natural gas.

Livestock includes animals that provide pork and beef. Because these are staple foods in most American diets, they provide among the more reliable pattern trends for trading. Pork bellies, lean hogs, and live cattle are all examples of tradable livestock commodities.

Softs are comprised of both food and fiber types of commodities. Many of these are deemed to be exotic since they are grown in other countries and parts of the earth. Among the soft markets that you can trade are sugar, coffee, cocoa, cotton, orange juice, and lumber.

Common Stock

Common stocks are shares in an underlying company that represent equity ownership in the corporation. They are also known as ordinary shares. These are securities in which individuals invest their capital. Common stock is the opposite of preferred stock.

While common stock and preferred stock both represent ownership in the company, there are many important differences between the two. Should a company go bankrupt, common stock holders are only given their money after preferred stock owners, bond owners, and creditors. Yet, common stock performs well, typically seeing greater levels of price appreciation than does preferred stock.

Common stock typically comes with voting rights, another feature that preferred stock does not have. These votes are used in electing the board of directors at the company's annual meeting, as well as in determining such things as company strategy, stock splits, policies, mergers and acquisitions, and the sale of the company. Preemptive rights in common stocks refer to owners with these rights being allowed to keep the same proportion of ownership in the company' stock, even if it issues additional stock.

Common stocks do not always pay dividends to share holders, as preferred stocks typically do. The dividends of common stocks are not pre-set or fixed. This means that the dividend returns are not completely predictable. Instead, they are based on a company's reinvestment policies, earnings results, and practices of the market in the valuing of the stock shares themselves.

Common shares have various other benefits. They are typically less expensive than are preferred stock shares. They are more heavily traded and readily available as well. The spreads between the buying and selling prices on them tend to be tighter as a result. Common stocks generally provide capital appreciation as the price of the shares rises over time, assuming that the company continues to do well and meet or exceed expectations. Dividends are often paid to common share holders when these things prove to be the case.

Common stocks can be purchased in any denominated amount. Round lots of common stocks are sold by even one hundred share amounts. This means that five hundred shares of common stock would be considered to be five lots of common stock.

Common stocks represent principally capital gains types of investments, as an investor is looking to buy them low and sell them at a higher price. This leads to a capital gain when the stock is sold at this greater level. The capital gain is the difference between the selling price and the purchasing price. Common stocks can also be cash flow types of investments when they pay a reliable stream of dividends every quarter. These income amounts are typically smaller than the one time amounts realized in capital gains, though they are obtained four times per year on a quarterly basis, or occasionally more often on a monthly basis.

Compound Interest

Compound interest represents interest which calculates on both the original principal amount as well as the interest that was accumulated previously during the loan or investment. Economists have called this miraculous phenomenon an interest on interest. It causes loans or invested deposits to increase at a significantly faster pace than only simple interest, the opposite of compound interest. Simple interest proves to be interest that calculates on just the principal amount of money.

Compound interest accrues at an interest rate which determines how often the compounding occurs. The higher the compound interest rate turns out to be, the faster the principal will compound and the more compounding periods will occur. Consider an example of how effective compounding truly is. $100 that is compounded at a rate of 10% per year will turn out to be less than $100 which is compounded at only 5% but semi annually during the same length of time.

Compound interest is important to individuals as it is able to take a few dollars worth of savings now and transform them into significant money throughout lifetimes. Investors do not need an MBA or a Wall Street background in order to benefit from this principle. Practically all investments earn compounding interest if the owners leave these earnings in the investment account over the long term.

This form of interest cuts both ways on the receiving and paying sides. When individuals are saving and investing money, it helps them grow the amount faster. When they are borrowing and paying the same interest on the debt, it grows against them faster. Individuals who are saving wish their money to compound as often as they can. Individuals who are borrowing wish it to compound as infrequently as possible. Savers are better off if they are able to compound quarterly instead of annually while just the opposite is true for borrowers.

For people who are compounding their investments, time works on their side. Money that grows at a rate of 6% each year doubles every 12 years. This means that it increases to four times as much as the original amount in only 24 years. For individuals paying compound interest, time is similarly working against them. Credit card companies utilize this principle to keep their card owners in debt forever by encouraging them to only make minimum monthly payments on the bills.

Thanks to compounding, a smaller amount of money that a person adds to an account upfront is more valuable than a larger sum of money he or she adds decades later. This cuts both ways. By paying down principal on a credit card with an extra $5 per month, the amount of compound interest individuals pay on a 14% interest rate credit card decreases by $1,315 over ten years. This is true even though they have paid only $600 in extra payments over this amount of time.

Anyone can make the miracle of compounding work for them. The idea works the same whether individuals are investing $100 or $100 million instead. Millionaires have greater ranges of investment choices. Even relatively poor people can compound their interest to increase their original amount and double their money as often as possible.

Compounding interest means that participants have to give up using some dollars today in order to obtain a greater benefit from them in the future. The little money may be missed now, but the rewards for the more significant amounts in the future will more than make up for the little sacrifice the individual makes now. Financial planners have claimed that the difference between poverty and financial comfort in the future amounts to even a few dollars in savings each week invested now rather than later.

Constructive Eviction

Constructive eviction is a backdoor way of evicting a tenant. It is not done through legal means because of a tenant failing to pay rent or seriously breaking the property rules. It is instead the process of a landlord making a rental uninhabitable for the tenant. Though the term sounds positive, it is quite the opposite. Landlords who engage in this type of eviction are failing to carry out their legal obligations.

For constructive eviction to take place, a residential rental property must deteriorate into enough disrepair that it becomes very difficult or near impossible to live in the property. It could also be that the landlord allows a condition to exist that makes inhabiting the home or apartment intolerable. As the condition becomes so severe that the property is no longer fit to live in, the tenant is forced to leave. An uninhabitable property exists in a state that compels the renter to move away, or to be constructively evicted. Because the renter is incapable of completely utilizing and possessing the property, he or she has been evicted technically.

There are a number of way in which a tenant could be a victim of constructive eviction. The landlord might turn off the electricity, gas, or water utilities. The owner might disregard an environmental problem such as toxic mold or flaking off lead paint and not properly clean it. He or she could also not fix leaking roofs. This causes water damage to walls and eventually leads to mold. The owners could block the unit entrance or change the locks. They might do something extreme such as take out sinks or toilets from the property as well. When the conditions deteriorate to the point that tenants abandon the rental then constructive eviction has occurred.

A landlord might engage in this type of unethical behavior because of rental controls. Many cities limit the amount by which rent can be increased. They may also allow the tenant to remain in the rental with an automatically renewing lease so long as they fulfill the contract obligations.

Tenants have the ability to fight back against this type of eviction. This starts with providing the owner a notice in writing of the constructive eviction. The landlord must be given a fair amount of time to address the issue. This may not translate to an instant repair that happens in 24 hours. Many repairs require more time to have completed. Water and gas leaks are examples of these. Still the repairs have to be done in a time frame that is reasonable.

Renters who find themselves in living conditions that are poor should take pictures. They also should invite independent inspectors to examine the property. These types of inspectors come from the permit or building department, as well as from the area health department.

When landlords are unwilling to address the uninhabitable living conditions in a reasonable time frame after having been given fair written notice, renters have rights. They are usually allowed to leave the property without having to pay rent that would still be owed according to the rental or lease agreement. In general, tenants have to move away from the property while they begin the legal process of terminating the lease and suing the owner for damages.

It is often better to compel the owner to make the necessary repairs or to address the issues that are creating the uninhabitable living conditions on the property in the first place. This is easier in cities and states that have strong legal enforcement of the landlord obligations. New York City and state are an example of places in the United States that make it difficult for owners to practice constructive eviction by requiring that they fulfill their maintenance duties.

Consumer Price Index (CPI)

The Consumer Price Index, also known by its acronym of CPI, actually measures changes that take place over time in the level of the pricing of various consumer goods and services that American households buy. The Bureau of Labor Statistics in the U.S. says that the Consumer Price Index is a measurement of the over time change in the prices that urban consumers actually pay for a certain grouping of consumer goods and services.

This consumer price index is not literal in the sense of what inflation really turns out to be. Instead, it is a statistical estimate that is built utilizing the costs of a basket of sample items that are supposed to be representative for the entire economy. These goods and services' prices are ascertained from time to time. In actual practice, both sub indices such as clothing, and even sub-sub indices, such as men's dress shirts, are calculated for varying sub-categories of services and goods. These are then taken and added together to create the total index. The different goods are assigned varying weights as shares of the total amount of the expenditures of consumers that the index covers.

Two essential pieces of information are necessary to build the consumer price index. These are the weighting data and the pricing data. Weighting data comes from estimates of differing kinds of expenditure shares as a percentage of the entire expenditure that the index covers. Sample household expenditure surveys are sourced to figure what the weightings should be. Otherwise, the National Income and Product Accounts estimates of expenditures on consumption are utilized. Pricing data is gathered from a sampling of goods and services taken from a sample range of sales outlets in varying locations and at a sampling of times.

The consumer price index is figured up monthly in the United States. Some other countries determine their CPI's on a quarterly basis. The different components of the consumer price index include food, clothing, and housing, all of which are weighted averages of the sub-sub indices. The CPI index literally compares the prices of one month with the prices in the reference month.

Consumer Price Index is only one of a few different pricing indices that the majority of national statistical agencies calculate. Inflation is figured up using the yearly percentage changes in the underlying consume price index. Uses of this CPI can include adjusting real values of pensions, salaries, and wages for inflation's effects, as well as for monitoring costs, and showing alterations in actual values through deflating the monetary magnitudes. The CPI and US National Income and Product Accounts prove to be among the most carefully followed of economic indicators.

Cost of living index is another measurement that is generated based on the consumer price index. It demonstrates how much consumer expenditures need to adjust to compensate for changes in prices. This details how much consumers need to keep up a constant standard of living.

Cost of Living Index

The Cost of Living Index refers to a price index that was created so that businesses and individuals are able to compare and contrast the cost of living relative to other cities, regions, countries, and times. This theoretical index takes the measure of variations in the costs of different key goods and services. It also permits substitutions with other similar goods when prices fluctuate.

One thing that is interesting regarding this Cost of Living Index is that there is not only a single methodology and index that reveals the national (or international) cost of living. One of the most widely used systems for these indices is known as the Konüs Index. These formats utilize an expenditure function like those employed in considering anticipated compensating variation.

In the United States, the most widely recognized and cited version of the Cost of Living Index was developed and is continuously maintained by the C2ER Council for Community and Economic Research. It first appeared in 1968. This version has proven to be the most consistent index for sourcing city to city cost-based comparisons in the United States. Their COLI data is widely recognized by such American governmental organizations as the U.S. Bureau of Labor Statistics and the U.S. Census Bureau. Similarly the President's Council of Economic Advisors utilizes it routinely. Private national media outlets including CNN Money, U.S. News and World Report, Forbes, Kiplinger's, ABC News, and countless others reference this index for the cost of living purposes. This makes it the closest possible thing to a nationally recognized and utilized COLI.

The reason for the C2ER COLI success centers on their entirely transparent methodology for creating and their locally sourcing of data. Users of the index know precisely how they compile it. They have an Advisory Board made up of government officials and academic researchers which reviews their methodology and data continuously. This helps to explain why this COLI finds reference use within the Census Bureau Statistical Abstract of the United States. As the C2ER publishes it quarterly and collects data on local levels from more than 300 different independent researchers, this represents the only locally-based and –sourced Cost of

Living Index compiled on the United States.

The firm employs more than 60 goods and services within the index's underlying data. They precisely select these different representative goods and services in order to take into consideration the various consumer categories of spending. They assign weights for the various costs utilizing data from government surveys citing executive and professional households' spending habits. Each item becomes priced at a fixed point in time for every locality utilizing specifications which are standardized.

A number of characteristics set this particular renowned COLI apart from its various inferior competitors. The data is provided for both county and large city MSA metropolitan statistical areas. They organize it by six different categories. These include housing, food, utilities, health care, transportation, and miscellaneous services and goods. Naturally C2ER offer the composite index as their primary one. The data comes out quarterly, no later than three months following its collection, so it is both fresh and relevant. Besides all of the government organizations which rely on their data and COLI in general, the Brookings Institution and Bankrate.com also cite their well-regarded methodology.

All of the various mainstream cost of living indexes rely on the theory which the Russian economist A. A. Konüs developed. The theory is only somewhat hampered by the assumption that the consumers act as optimizers to receive the maximum utility possible out of the money which they possess and can spend. The weakness is that this standard baseline assertion does not always work out to be the case in practice.

Credit Bureaus

Credit bureaus are agencies that collect financial information. They go by different names in various countries around the world. In the United Kingdom they are known as credit reference agencies. In Australia, the bureaus are called credit reporting bodies. India knows their credit agencies as credit information companies.

Within the United States, these organizations are called consumer reporting agencies. Whatever name they go by, they all serve the same function. The bureaus gather information from banks and other financial sources to deliver consumer credit information about individual consumers.

The U.S. consumer reporting agencies are governed by the Fair Credit Reporting Act. Other laws that regulate the activities of the bureaus are the Fair and Accurate Credit Transactions Act, the Fair Credit Billing Act, the Fair Credit Reporting Act, and Regulation B. These acts attempt to safeguard consumers against unfair practices and mistakes made by the data providers and the credit reporting agencies themselves.

The U.S. has two separate government organizations who oversee the credit bureaus and their data suppliers. These are the FTC and the OCC. Primary oversight of the credit reporting agencies as they deal with consumers belongs to the Federal Trade Commission. The banks are monitored for all of the information that they provide the reporting agencies by the Office of the Controller of the Currency. This government agency supervises, regulates, and charters all of the national banks and any information they turn over to the consumer credit reporting agencies.

Three main credit reporting bureaus dominate nearly all credit reporting in the U.S. These are Experian, Equifax, and TransUnion. None of these three agencies are owned by government entities. All of them exist as companies seeking to make a profit and are traded publically. They are carefully monitored for fairness by the government provided oversight organizations.

The consumer reporting agencies operate through a vast network with the credit card issuing companies, banks, and other financial entities with which individuals have accounts. All of these ties ensure that credit account information and histories show up on the credit reports of one, two, or even all of the bureaus.

The credit bureaus compile all of this information into a consumer credit report. They each then utilize proprietary trade secret formulas to determine every individual's FICO credit score. Each of the three bureaus formulates its own score that is different from that of its competitors. They also come up with educational credit score numbers which are often vastly different from the official scores.

Consumers do not have to settle for educational credit scores. They have the rights to see what is on their credit reports. Each and every year, individuals are able to obtain an official credit report from each of the three credit bureaus. This can be done by going to the government mandated website AnnualCreditReport.com.

Besides this, consumers are allowed to go to the websites of the three main consumer reporting agencies and order credit reports and scores from them directly. The only way to get the official credit score is to pay for and order it from the credit bureaus themselves. These are not provided in the annual free reports. Experian and Equifax offer all three credit reports in a single convenient to view document.

Sometimes the credit bureaus will make mistakes with individuals' credit reports. When this happens, it is important to get in touch with the credit bureau itself in order to dispute any information that is inaccurate. These organizations also should be contacted directly if there is concern about fraud so that they can place a security alert or fraud alert on the person's credit report.

Credit History

Credit history is an official record that shows the company or personal history of borrowing and paying back loans. This history provides business or personal identifying information, a record of credit that the individual or company has, and negative elements such as bankruptcies and late payments.

It describes how individuals use their money and finances. It lists out the number of credit cards, loans and other obligations, and bills that a consumer has. It keeps records of whether they pay these bills in a timely fashion. The credit history information is compiled as companies send in data on credit cards and loans to one of the three main credit bureaus. These are Experian, Equifax, and TransUnion. They act as the gatekeepers of credit history.

These companies compile all of this information on credit and bills into a file called a credit report. This credit report is the repository of all an individual's credit history. It contains a great deal of personal information that starts with the owner's name, social security number, and address. All credit cards and loans are itemized out and detailed. It states the total money a person owes. Finally, credit reports put together a profile on the individuals as to whether they pay their bills late or on time.

Credit history and credit reports are important for individuals. Businesses will not loan out money to people until they know all about them and their spending and borrowing habits and past. Businesses find all of this information on personal credit history in these credit reports and then make decisions as to whether they will extend credit in the form of a credit card or make a loan to the applicant.

Some employers choose to examine a candidate's credit report along with a job application. Insurance companies also consider it when they are determining rates of their customers. Even cell phone and utility companies often look it up when they are deciding how much a person will need to pay in deposits to start service.

Credit history is also used to create a credit score. Credit scores are numbers that the three credit reporting bureaus maintain for individuals using their credit history. If the credit history is good, then the credit score will be as well. Individuals can see their credit history and obtain their credit reports for free every year. Credit scores are not available unless people pay for them.

High credit scores convey a good credit history. Lower credit scores refer to a poor credit history for an individual. Each of the three credit bureau companies will have a slightly different score for a person. High credit scores range from 700-850. Low credit scores start from 300 to 600.

Credit history as shown in a personal credit report is very important to know. Each of the three companies is required to send individuals their credit report every year showing personal credit history on demand. Individuals are able to request this at no charge by going to AnnualCreditReport.com.

There are other companies that advertise offers to provide credit scores for free along with free credit reports. These are usually promotional offers that require individuals to sign up for a monthly service of some type in order to qualify for them. Such offers are often monthly credit monitoring services for a fee. As a rule, a person will generally have to pay something to obtain his or her credit scores.

Credit Ratings Agencies

Credit Ratings Agencies are those companies whose purpose is to consider and report on the financial strength which firms and government agencies demonstrate. They report on national as well as international corporations and agencies in this capacity. Their reports are most interested in the ability of the entities in question to fulfill their obligations for both principal and interest repayments of their bonds and other kinds of debts. Besides this, the various ratings agencies carefully examine and review the conditions and terms on every debt issue.

The end result of the agencies' work is to release a credit rating on both the debt issues in particular and the debt issuers more generally. When they agencies have high confidence that the issuer will be able to meet their debt servicing of principal and interest as promised, they will issue a high credit rating. When the opposite is true, the credit rating will be lower. It is entirely possible for a particular issue of debt to receive a differing credit rating from the issuer. This heavily depends on the particular terms of the issuer.

The impacts of these debt issue ratings are enormous in the industry and for the specific issuers in question. Those debt issues that obtain the best credit ratings will receive the most attractive interest rates from the credit markets. This is because the confidence of investors in an entity's capability of making their various payment obligations comes down to the credit ratings agencies review, analyses and especially ratings. Since the interest rates which investors demand for a specific debt issue will be inversely correlated to the borrower's particular creditworthiness, weaker borrowers will have to pay more while the stronger ones will enjoy paying less.

In this way, the credit ratings agencies act on behalf of businesses in much the same capacity as the consumer credit bureaus do for individual consumers. Such credit scores which the credit bureaus develop for individual people will greatly impact the interest rates at which individuals are able to borrow money.

The downside to these credit ratings agencies and their work is that they have been made the scapegoat for company and government defaults in recent years. Their research quality in particular has been the target of heavy criticism from observers and analysts who point out companies which they rated highly suddenly collapsed. Governments in Europe on which they provided high credit ratings defaulted or almost defaulted on their debts, as with Greece in particular.

This caused third party observers to argue that the various credit ratings agencies are actually poor at financial forecasting, at uncovering growing and negative trends for the debt issuers they follow, and also are overly late in revising down their ratings. Besides this, critics point to the many conflicts of interest of the ratings agencies. This is because the debt issuers are able to pick out and pay the ratings agencies for the reviews of their bonds. In a survey conducted in 2008, 11 percent of the various investment professionals surveyed by the CFA Institute responded that they had observed personally instances where the major ratings agencies had actually upgraded their given ratings on bonds when they were pressured by the debt issuers in question.

There are only three firms today which dominate the space, and this is part of the problem. The Wall Street Journal provided the ratings shares of the big 3 agencies in their 2011 report. Of the 2.8 million ratings they issue collectively (with the other seven minor agencies), S&P 500 controls the greatest market share with 42.2 percent. Moody's holds 36.9 percent of the market. Fitch rounds out the top three with 17.9 percent.

The article claimed that fully 95 percent of all revenues in this industry were earned by the big three. Only 2.9 percent of the ratings issued came from the other seven firms. The other seven credit ratings agencies were A.M. Best, DBRS, Japan Credit Rating Agency, Rating and Investment Info., Egan-Jones Ratings, Morningstar Credit Ratings, and Kroll Bond Rating Agency.

Between the top two issuers Moody's and Standard & Poor's, they provide ratings for roughly 80 percent of all municipal and corporate bond issues. They are typically regarded as a level higher than Fitch. One particular example speaks volumes. While Egan-Jones had downgraded the U.S. Federal government debt to the second highest rating years earlier, it was ignored largely by the markets and world. When Standard & Poor's took the same action by downgrading the Federal government of the United States debt to AA+ on August 5th of 2011, this shook the world bond, currency, and stock markets. It demonstrates the clout S&P and Moody's especially enjoy over all of their various credit ratings agencies rivals.

Credit Repair Organizations

Credit repair organizations are those which offer to assist individuals with clearing up their credit report and improving their credit scores. While a number of them are legitimate operations, others can be scams. Such credit repair clinics often charge exorbitant prices to perform services that individuals can do for themselves. There were enough problems with fraud or unfulfilled promises from these organizations that Congress created a law to reduce abuse. This is known as the Credit Repair Organizations Act.

Many credit repair organizations will offer to have incorrect information removed from the credit file of an individual. Consumers can do this themselves according to the provisions of the Fair Credit Reporting Act. Others will promise to take off information that is negative but correct from the files. Generally this takes seven years or longer for such information to go away if it is accurate.

The credit repair clinics have a strategy to challenge all items in a customer's file. These could be neutral, negative, or positive. They do this hoping that they can overwhelm the credit bureaus so that they will simply take off information rather than verify it first. The problem with this tactic is that credit bureaus are allowed under the Fair Credit Reporting Act to dismiss frivolous challenges. There are cases where the credit bureau may remove such information. The problem is that correct information often shows up again in one to two months as the original creditors will report negative information again.

Credit repair organizations also offer to have court judgments and existing debt balances taken off of credit files. They can do this by negotiating partial or whole payments with the creditors in exchange for taking negative information away from the credit report. While these are legitimate negotiation tactics, individuals can do this without having to pay credit repair clinics for the service.

Another suggestion that such credit repair organizations may make to consumer clients is to obtain a secured credit card from a bank which offers them. These are simply credit cards that individuals use after putting a deposit in an account at their bank. These secured credit card lists that the credit repair clinics offer are not proprietary. Individuals can find the same information for free or very little online.

Congress attempted to curb abuses from credit repair clinics with their Credit Repair Organizations Act. It regulates these clinics that are for profit. The law states that these credit repair outfits must provide individuals with written statements of rights provided by the FCR Act. They must correctly present what they are and are not able to accomplish. They are not allowed to charge and collect fees until they render all services which they promised.

The credit repair clinic must provide a contract in writing. They have to allow consumers to cancel the contracts within three days of signing them. Consumers must provide such cancellations in writing. All contracts that do not follow the Credit Repair Organizations Act become void. Consumers can not sign away any of their rights.

There are unethical credit repair clinics which have found a means to get around the law. They incorporate themselves as not for profit organizations. This makes it easier for them to offer poor or limited results and to take customers' money. They also find it simpler to perform the same services that consumers can do for themselves this way.

Credit Report

A credit report is an individual or business' credit history. This includes their record of borrowing and repaying money in the past. It similarly covers data pertaining to any late payments made or bankruptcies that have been declared. In some countries, credit reports are also referred to as credit reputations.

When an American like you completes a credit application for a bank, a credit card company, or a retail store, this information is directly sent on to one of the three main credit bureaus. These are Experian, Trans Union, and Equifax. These credit bureaus then match up your name, identification, address, and phone number on the application for such credit with the data that they keep in their bureau's files. Because of this match up process, it is essential that lenders, creditors, and other parties always provide exactly correct information to the credit bureaus.

Such information in these files at the three major credit bureaus is then utilized by lenders like credit card companies in order to decide if you are deserving of having credit issued to you by the creditor. Another way of putting this is that they decide how likely that you will be to pay back these debts. Such willingness to pay back a debt is usually indicated by the timeliness of prior payments to other lenders. Such lenders will prefer to see the debt obligations of individual consumers, such as yourself, paid on time every month.

The second element considered in a lender offering loans or credit to individuals like you is based on your actual income. Higher incomes generally lead to greater amounts of credit being accessible. Still, lenders look at both willingness, as shown in the credit report and prior payment history, along with ability, as shown by income, in deciding whether or not to extend you credit.

Credit reports have become even more significant in light of risk based pricing. Practically all lenders of the financial services industry rely on credit reports to determine what the annual percentage rate and grace period of repayment of a loan or offer of credit will be. Other obligations of the contract are similarly based on this credit report.

In the past, a great deal of discussion has gone on considering the information contained in the credit reports. Scientific studies done on the issue have determined that for the most part, this credit report information is extremely accurate. Such credit bureaus also have their own authorized studies of fifty-two million credit reports that show that the information contained therein is right a vast majority of the time.

Congress has heard testimony from the Consumer Data Industry Association that in fewer than two percent of credit report issue cases have there been data which had to be erased because it was wrong. In the few cases where these did exist, more than seventy percent of such disputes are handled in fourteen days or less. More than ninety-five percent of consumers with disputes report being satisfied with the resolution.

Credit Score

Credit Score refers to a number generated by the credit bureaus to represent the creditworthiness of an individual. The credit bureaus possess literally from hundreds to thousands of distinct lines worth of information on each person with a credit profile. This makes it extremely difficult for lending institutions to go through it all. Since they lack the man hours to carefully peruse each applicant's credit reports personally, the majority of financial institutions which lend money employ these credit scores rather than tediously read through credit reports on applicants.

These Credit Scores are actually numbers that a computer program generates after crawling through an individual's credit report. Such programs seek out certain fundamentals, patterns, and so-called warning flags in any credit report and history. They then generate a credit score based on what they find. Lenders love these scores since they can be basically interpreted by a consistent set of comparative rules.

Consider the following examples. Lending institutions might automatically approve any application that comes with an associated 720 credit score or higher. Those profiles with 650 to 720 would likely be approved but with a greater interest rate. Applications with credit scores below 650 might simply be rejected. The computer is consistent and fair using these standards, so no one is treated in a discriminatory way relative to any other applicant.

Federal laws require that each individual be granted a free credit report annually from every one of the big three credit bureaus Experian, Trans Union, and Equifax. This does not mean that anyone is required to hand out free credit scores. In fact there is no such thing as a truly free credit score offer. There are scores provided in exchange for signing up for trial membership services in things like credit monitoring services. In general though, individuals pay for their credit scores from each of the major credit bureaus.

The particulars of a Credit Score are interesting. It is always a three digit formatted number that ranges from 300 to 850. These become created using one of a variety of mathematical algorithms that work off of both the individuals' credit profiles and their credit report's particular information.

This score is crafted with the intention of predicting risk to the lenders, not to benefit the person it covers. It is particularly concerned with the chances of an individual going delinquent on any credit obligations within the next 24 months after the score has been issued.

It is a common misnomer among many individuals that there is only one credit scoring model in the country. There are countless models that exist. It is only the FICO credit score that matters in nearly all cases though. This is because fully 90 percent of financial institutions within the United States rely on FICO credit scores in making their decisions on to whom they will extend credit and at what interest rate.

The higher the FICO score these algorithms generate, the lower the risk is to the various lenders. What makes matters more confusing is that there is not only one FICO credit score in existence for every adult American. Each of the three major bureaus generates its own particular score. Since 2009, consumers are only able to view two of their credit scores, those from both Trans Union and Equifax. This is because Experian chose to terminate its myFICO.com arrangements in 2009. Experian does not share their proprietary credit scores with consumers any longer.

Five different significant categories make up the FICO Credit Score. These are payment history (35 percent of the total component), Amounts owed (30 percent), length of credit history (15 percent), types of credit used (10 percent), and new credit inquiries and accounts opened (10 percent).

Crypto Currency

A crypto currency turns out to be a virtual currency. These alternative currencies deploy cryptography as a means of security. It makes them extremely hard to counterfeit since this security feature is complex. An element that consistently defines the various crypto currencies and simultaneously endears them to users is their independent nature. They cannot be issued nor controlled by any of the global central banks or world monetary authorities. The theory is that this makes it difficult (if not outright impossible) for governments to manipulate or control such currencies.

Unfortunately for the governments of the world, this somewhat anonymous characteristic of the global crypto currencies also makes them an ideal vehicle for illegal and otherwise unethical activities. Among these are drug dealing, tax evading, and money laundering carried on around the world.

The world's original (and still leading) crypto currency proved to be Bitcoin. This was the first of the alternative currencies that caught on with the general and investing public. A mysterious individual or group of individuals who go only by the pseudonym of Satoshi Nakamoto created and launched Bitcoin back in 2009. These BTC (as they are abbreviated) must be mined in a tedious process which involves solving complex computer algorithmic problems. There is a maximum limit of 21 million to the total number of BTC which may be created. As of September of 2015, already 14.6 million of these Bitcoins had been mined and were circulating. The success of Bitcoin has been so vast that other competing crypto currencies have been spawned over the years.

The greatest and most successful of these is Ethereum, or Ether tokens. Others that have appeared include Litecoin, PPCoin, and Namecoin. These descendants of Bitcoin are often referred to as altcoins. This name is a derivative of the phrase bitcoin alternative. All of these crypto currencies have at least one thing in common. They all rely on a decentralized control. This stands out in direct contrast to the centralized banking systems of the mainstream traditional currencies.

There are a number of advantages and also some disadvantages to the major crypto currencies and this ground breaking technology. On the positive side, the crypto currencies enable simpler, cheaper, faster transfers of funds between one party and another in a commercial transaction. The transfers of funds occur utilizing both private and public keys to provide greater security.

The transfers happen with the lowest of possible processing and transaction costs. This has disrupted traditional banking and finance significantly. Individuals who transact in a crypto currency are able to side step the hefty middle man fee of financial institutions such as banks with their wire transfer costs, or with money transfer services like Western Union and Money Gram. These last two services charge upwards of ten percent transfer fees.

The great brilliance of Bitcoin and the other major crypto currencies lies in their block chain technology which acts as storage for the transaction ledger online. In fact all transactions in the BTC technology and currency which have ever happened are maintained in the block chain ledger database. Major banks like JP Morgan Chase have already invested heavily in initiatives to reduce the transaction costs of payment processing and transfers utilizing especially the up and coming Ethereum crypto currency.

This does not mean that there are not downsides to the crypto currencies. As they lack a central offline repository, the balance of an online wallet can be completely wiped out by either the invasion of hackers who steal it or the advent of a single computer crash if owners do not backup their holdings with data copies. There is also the negative of the wildly gyrating volatility in the currencies, which can easily swing up or down by even ten or twenty percent in a single trading session or week. There have also been more than 40 instances of online hacking theft of the various Bitcoin exchanges and companies in the short decade of Bitcoin history.

Debit Card

Debit cards are plastic cards that function like a check and are easily utilized like a credit card. Debit cards are commonly one of two types, either branded Visa or Master Card. When you use such a debit card to pay for a purchase, then this amount is deducted immediately from your checking account. Both convenience and security features are included in the use of a debit card.

Debit cards provide tremendous convenience in their ease of use. No longer do you have to make sure that you are carrying enough money on you, or to take the time to write out a physical check while the long line waits impatiently behind you. Besides this ease of use, debit cards are accepted at literally millions of places around the country and the world.

Nowadays, they can be used for almost any purchase, such as lunches or dinners at restaurants, monthly bill payments, merchandise in retail stores, groceries, prescriptions, gas, online purchases, over the phone orders, and even fast food.

Debit cards' spending is easy to keep track of as well. The majority of such transactions are both deducted and posted to a checking account in twenty-four hours or less. This allows for you to conveniently monitor your constantly updated transaction record and balance either over the phone or the bank or card issuer's website. Besides this, debit cards also offer statements, much like credit cards, that outline all purchases made, with details on the name of the merchant, date, location, and amount of transaction.

Debit cards offer another benefit in their security provisions. These cards include free fraud monitoring that helps to find and stop activity that is suspicious with your debit card. They also come with policies of zero liability that protect you from charges that you did not make or authorize. Fraudulently taken out funds are guaranteed to be returned to your account. The vast majority of debit cards also come with the security feature of three digit security codes that allow you to confirm your identity for both phone and Internet orders and purchases.

Debit cards allow two ways for completing in person transactions. One of these is through swiping the card and then signing the receipt issued by the merchant representative. The other is via using a pad with your PIN, or personal identification code, after the card is swiped.

A final benefit that you gain from a debit card is that most of them provide rewards that are earned simply by utilizing them. These are earned in one of two ways. With Visa Debit cards, you are able to receive discounts from some merchants who provide these special price breaks for the holders of Visa cards.

Other debit cards provide extras rewards programs. These rewards programs pay you back with some type of reward for every purchase that you make. These can be cash rebates or more commonly awards that are earned through the collection of such points.

Debt Consolidation

Debt consolidation is combining all of an individual's personal debts into a single larger debt. When people go though debt consolidation, they obtain one loan which they then use to pay down all smaller loans or outstanding debts. The idea is that this provides consumers with only a single payment that they make once per month. This is supposed to be simpler for consumers to pay and manage.

A main goal with debt consolidation is to obtain a lower interest rate. The monthly payment generally becomes lower through the process as well. Despite the fact that the payment is lower, the debt can be repaid faster. The lower interest rate makes this possible.

Debt consolidation is different from debt settlement. In debt settlement, higher outstanding bills are negotiated to lower more manageable amounts. In debt consolidation, individuals fully pay off all of their bills. There are no bad impacts on credit history and reports as a result of the consolidation process.

Consumers pursue debt consolidation through either an unsecured or a secured loan. An unsecured loan does not involve any collateral. This means that no personal assets back the loan. The lender extends the loan because the individual pledges to repay it. A credit card is a prime example of an unsecured loan. Many credit cards offer debt consolidation with a lower promotional interest rate to their customers. In general, the rates are higher on unsecured loans. This is because the risk is greater for the lender with an unsecured loan than with a secured loan.

With a secured loan, individuals receive the debt consolidation funds because they pledge an asset. These assets that secure the loan are usually a car or a home. Car loans and mortgages are both secured forms of loans. The downside to a secured loan is that a lender can seize the asset if consumers fall behind on the loan.

Debt consolidation with a secured loan happens through a variety of different types of loans. Among the more popular secured debt consolidation loans is a second mortgage home loan or a home equity line of credit. It is also possible to obtain a debt consolidation loan with a 401k. In this type of loan, retirement funds are the asset that underlies the loan. Insurance policies allow owners to take loans against the value in the policy as well.

Annuities are another vehicle that can sometimes be borrowed against. A number of special financing companies also issue loans against lottery winnings or lawsuit claims. In each of these cases, the element in common is that the asset secures the debt consolidation loan.

There are both pros and cons to consolidating bills with an unsecured loan. The biggest difficulty with these types of loans is obtaining them. Unsecured loans require fantastic credit in order to qualify. The interest rates are typically higher than those on secured loans as well. Still the rates are often lower than the ones charged by high interest credit cards. If these consolidation rates are not substantially lower than those of the bills on the debt consolidation loan, then it may not make a difference in the payments and payoff time-frame.

Debt consolidation loans that rely on credit card balance transfers can present problems. It is important to be aware of what happens after the promotional balance expires. The new interest rate may be so high that the loan does not provide any benefits over the terms of the old debts. There are commonly transfer fees with these credit card balance transfers. These can eat up a part of the savings that the debt consolidation should provide.

Debt Forgiveness

Debt Forgiveness refers to the action of writing off all or some of a debt which a debtor has outstanding and usually simply cannot hope to repay. This act of forgiving debt can occur for the purpose of reducing the total sum of loss which the lender will otherwise incur because of defaults. From time to time, this idea has been pursued to strengthen the national economy in countries that would rather write down their debt against resources they borrowed on in prior years.

There are definite advantages for a lender or creditor in choosing to pursue debt forgiveness with their borrowers. When they grant this forgiveness of debt, they can save huge amounts of resources and wasted time trying to collect on a bad debt. This means that such resources are then freed up for more productive activities going forward. In a number of countries, the regulations and laws concerning credit and debt permit the creditor to claim an associated tax deduction for at least some if not all of the debt which they forgive. This enables them to additionally reduce the revenue loss from the anticipated income stream of the borrower's payments.

In these scenarios, debtors receive the opportunity to escape from part of even all of the debt in question. This can significantly help them to ease their financial case especially after they have suffered from various dramatic financial setbacks and can no longer honor the previously negotiated debts. One downside is that many sovereign governments choose to tax any and all debt forgiveness as real income. This means that while the debtor may enjoy a temporary form of relief from the burdensome debts, they may become categorized according to a higher tax bracket at least for that particular year. This could lead to a hefty tax bill which they cannot settle with the taxing authorities. It can create a whole host of new problems in place of the older and now forgiven ones.

The process of debt forgiveness even happens between one nation and another creditor country. It always helps to consider concrete examples of these concepts to better understand them. Nations which are recovering form devastating natural disasters could not be able to pay debts or even interest owed on them for a few years after such a disaster occurs. Instead of destroy the nation's fragile economy at that point and time, creditor nations will often decide instead to simply write off the loan. This is not an atypical event when it is clear that the economy of the nation will collapse otherwise, especially as this often impacts the entire global economy should it occur.

It is not important as to whether such debt forgiveness is actually applied to individuals, companies, or nations. The process is generally the same. It is also rarely pursued before all other potential avenues are fully explored. Usually what will happen is that debt will not be written down or off if there is any practical possibility that the financial condition for the debtor in question will improve in an acceptable to the creditor time frame. Yet in the end, this debt forgiveness will typically prove to be the most intelligent and ultimately practical form of action if the debtor's financial condition does not look like it will improve any time soon so that the debtor can actually resume their debt and interest payments in an reasonable time frame going forward.

Debt Relief

Debt relief refers to the effective reorganizing of any form of debt so that the indebted party experiences at least some debt forgiveness. This could be complete or partial relief of debt from a large or even overwhelming burden. It is possible for it to take a wide range of scenarios. Relief might be offered in the form of lowering the aggregate principal in whole or in part. It might also be accomplished through lengthening the loan term or reducing the total interest rate and payments of loans which are due.

Debt relief also relates to debt forgiveness in order to stop the growth of the principal or at least to slow it down. This can be done for groups ranging from individual people to companies or multinational corporations to entire nations. From the days of the ancient world up to the 1800s, it primarily pertained to individual and household debt. This especially meant freeing of slaves from indebtedness or forgiving agriculture debts.

In the last years of the 1900s, the use of the phrase changed to cover mostly debt of the Third World. This began with the skyrocketing debt from the Latin American Debt Crisis that included such countries as Mexico and Argentina. By the early years of the 2000s, the phrase had greater application to individuals in wealthy countries that had been ravaged by housing and credit bubbles.

Debt relief in the 20th century came to apply to nations after the devastating effects of the First World War. Those debt payments from the allies of the United states were suspended in the dark depths of the Great Depression from 1931. Finland was the only country to repay these debts in full. Germany also received debt relief of its war reparation burdens from the United States, Britain, and France with the Agreement on German External Debts in 1953. This represented one of the first large scale applications of debt relief on an international scale.

By the 1990s, debt relief had become an urgent need for those under-developed nations which were heavily in debt. This became a mission in the 1990s for a number of Christian organizations, Non Governmental Organizations focused on development, and others partners who worked in an enormous coalition which called itself Jubilee 2000. As part of the campaign to push for debt forgiveness and relief, there were demonstrations at meetings like the G8 Summit in Birmingham, England in 1998. This helped the agenda for debt relief to reach the radar of international organizations like the World Bank and IMF International Monetary Fund as well as Western developed nations' governments.

It actually became public policy through an initiative called the HIPC Heavily Indebted Poor Countries program. This initiative started out in order to offer consistent help in the form of debt relief to those most impoverished nations of the world. It worked strenuously to make certain that the money donated went for reduction of poverty and did not get siphoned off to infrastructure or military buildup programs.

This World Bank-supervised project involved conditions which were much like those accompanying loans from the World Bank and IMF International Monetary Fund. They mandated strict structural reforms that often involved privatizing public utilities including electricity and water. The prospective nations had to institute Poverty Reduction Strategies and demonstrate substantial macroeconomic stability for minimally a year.

In order to cut inflation, there were nations goaded into reducing their expenditures on important sectors such as education and health. The World Bank may have deemed the HIPC protocols a triumph for the twin goals of poverty and debt reduction, but many scholars and analysts offered significant criticisms of the program.

Despite critiques though, the HIPC became extended through the MDRI Multilateral Debt Relief Initiative. After the Gleneagles G8 meeting of 2005 in July, the wealthy creditor nations signed on to the MDRI. This provided full, complete elimination of all HIPC countries' multilateral debts which they owed to the IMF, World Bank, and African Development Bank.

Deed

A Deed refers to a legal document which allows for a real estate ownership transfer from one party to another. Within the document will always be the names of the new and old owners of the property as well as the legally binding description of said real estate. The document must be signed over by the individual who is selling the property to the buyer.

It is impossible to transfer ownership of a piece of real estate unless you have a document in writing. This is nearly always the deed. Interestingly enough, there is not simply one type of these deeds. There are quitclaim, warranty, grant, and transfer on death kinds of deeds in existence. Each of them has their own reason of use.

Quitclaim deeds are what many individuals regard as basic deeds. They simply transfer over any ownership stake an individual may have in a given property. These do not define the full percentage of the receiver's interest in the property however. They are often utilized by couples getting divorced. One of the aggrieved parties signs off on his or her full rights in the married couple's joint properties to the other party. This is particularly helpful when a lack of clarity exists on an interest in a property that one of the owners (like a spouse) has in his or her name. Quitclaims never absolve the forfeiting party from the co- responsibilities of the mortgage however.

These Quitclaim deeds are also employed when title searches discover that a prior owner or heir to an estate possesses a partial claim on the real estate in question. That individual is able to sign off on such a quitclaim deed in order to allow for the transfer of whatever interest remains to them in the said property.

Warranty deeds provide ownership transfer along with a good guarantee that the transferring party possesses clean title on the real estate. This means that the purchaser can have confidence in the property being completely free of ownership claims or liens. These deeds deliver a guarantee from the sellers that they will provide compensation to the purchasers should this pledge prove to be incorrect. It is also possible for warranty deeds to provide other guarantees that address other potential issues with the real estate transfer transaction.

Grant deeds are those kinds that imply certain pledges along with transferring the ownership of title to the property. These pledges might include that the title is not encumbered or has not previously transferred over to someone else.

Finally, TOD Transfer on Death deeds are much like regular formats of deeds. Their critical difference is that they only go into effect when the owner of the property in question dies. In other words, they permit property holders to will real estate to an heir without having to become involved in proceedings in probate court. Upon death, the deed-named beneficiary will immediately assume ownership of the real estate. This avoids any and all delays and probate paperwork.

Creating such TOD deeds is not any more difficult than completing normal deeds. The owner simply designates the beneficiary, signs said deed, has it notarized, and records it with the appropriate property records office for the given jurisdiction. Such deeds are permitted in 23 different states. These include Wyoming, Wisconsin, Washington, Virginia, South Dakota, Oregon, Oklahoma, Ohio, North Dakota, New Mexico, Nevada, Nebraska, Montana, Missouri, Minnesota, Kansas, Indiana, Illinois, Hawaii, Washington District of Columbia, Colorado, Arkansas, and Arizona.

Deeds are required by law to first be notarized (and sometimes also witnessed) before being filed in the area public records office. The appropriate local records office is typically called either a Land Registry Office, County Recorder's Office, or Register of Deeds. This office is typically located within the county courthouse.

Deed in Lieu of Foreclosure

A deed in lieu of foreclosure represents an alternative option to a standard foreclosure on a house. In this deed in lieu arrangement, the owner of the property decides to hand over the property in question to the lender on a completely voluntary basis. In exchange for agreeing to this, the lender cancels out the mortgage loan. The deed to the house becomes transferred from the owner to the lender. As part of this conciliatory arrangement, the mortgage lender guarantees that it will not start the foreclosure process on the owner. If there are any foreclosure actions that have already begun, the lender will also terminate these. It is up to the lender to decide if they will forgive any extra balance that the sale of the home does not cover.

There are some tax issues that can arise with a deed in lieu of foreclosure deal. One potential downside to this type of debt forgiveness involves the consequences of it with the IRS. Federal law in the United States requires creditors to file 1099C forms for tax purposes when they choose to forgive any loan balance that amounts to more than $600. This debt forgiveness is then considered to be income and it becomes a tax liability for the home owner.

Fortunately for many home owners during the financial crisis, Congress passed the Mortgage Forgiveness Debt Relief Act of 2007. This delivered tax relief on a number of loans that banks forgave in the years starting from 2007 till the end of 2013.

The main issue and advantage that a deed in lieu of foreclosure offers centers around this excess balance debt forgiveness. Anyone who enters into such a voluntary agreement should carefully review the contract to learn how the deficiency balance topic will be addressed. Sometimes the documents are not clear on this point.

In this case, the homeowner should take the deed in lieu document to a lawyer who specializes in property law. It is not inexpensive to have a lawyer review such a contract document. The money it can save the home owner in the future for signing a contract he or she does not understand and may suffer significantly from will make the fees seem reasonable by comparison.

There are a number of requirements in order for a deed in lieu of foreclosure to be accepted. First the house would have to be on the seller market for a minimum number of days. Ninety days is usual. There also may not be any liens on the house. The property typically could not be in the process of foreclosure already. Finally, the deed in lieu offer has to be voluntary on the part of the home owner.

Another option that can be pursued in place of this deed in lieu of foreclosure is a short sale. Short sales have the same requirements as do the deed in lieu arrangements with several additional stipulations. The home seller must be suffering from financial hardship. The home itself has to be offered at a reasonable price.

In an alternative short sale, the mortgage lender will consent to receiving a lesser amount from the sale than the remaining mortgage balance that the owner still owes. It is up to the bank and the contract if any additional balance which exists will be forgiven or not. The same tax issues apply if the lender agrees to forgive more than $600.

Defined Benefit Plan

A defined benefit plan is a pension plan that serves as a vehicle for retirement. These plans give owners who are retiring benefits that are already pre-determined when they are established. These plans turn out to be a win-win situation for all parties.

Employees like the set benefit towards retirement that this provides. Employers also appreciate particular features of the plan. An employer is able to make larger contributions with this type of plan than with a defined contribution plan. Businesses can deduct the amounts they contribute from their tax liabilities. These types of plans are more complicated than the defined contribution plans. This is what sets the two types of plans apart. Defined benefit plans are more expensive to set up and to maintain than are alternative employee benefit plans.

What makes these plans more helpful to employees is the contributor. Employers usually contribute the most to them. Cases exist where employees can make voluntary contributions of their own. Occasionally the plan requires employees to make contributions. Whoever contributes, the benefits delivered by the plan are limited. The IRS sets and changes these limits every few years.

There are numerous distinctive features to these types of plans. An advantage to defined benefit plans is that plan participants can be allowed to take a loan against the value of the plan. Distributions before the participant reaches 62 are usually not allowed while the employee is still working for the company. The employees with the defined benefit plans are allowed to participate in other retirement plans.

Businesses have certain requirements with these plans as well. Companies of all sizes can participate in one. They are able to offer other types of retirement plans as well. Participating companies need to have an actuary who is enrolled in the plan decide how much the funding levels should be. Businesses also may not decrease the plan benefits after they have set them.

There are many advantages to defined benefit plans. Companies can confer significant retirement benefits on employees in a small amount of time. Employees can earn these benefits in a similarly short time frame. Even early retirement does not eliminate the ability to access these benefits. Employers appreciate that they can put more into these plans than with alternatives plans Employees love the predictable dollar benefits that the plans deliver. They also are happy to have a retirement account whose benefits do not depend on investment returns.

The schedule for becoming vested in the money of this benefit account varies. It can be set up for immediate full vesting. Schedules for vesting can stretch to as long as seven years with defined benefit plans as well. Some employers use the flexibility with these accounts to provide an early retirement package. Offering special benefit packages for early retirement is achievable with defined benefit plans.

There are also several downsides to these types of plans. They are the most complicated plan to administer and run. Defined benefit plans are also the most expensive kind of retirement benefit plan that a company can offer.

The IRS penalizes companies that do not make their minimum contribution requirement for a year. They do this using an excise tax when the minimums are not met. Some companies may wish to make larger contributions to the plan than they need to do. They might be motivated by the larger tax breaks. If a company over contributes, than an excise tax also applies.

Defined Contribution Plans

Defined contribution plans turn out to be a specific type of retirement plan. In these, an employer's yearly dollar amount contribution to the plan is spelled out clearly. Accounts are established on an individual basis for all employees participating. The amounts that are credited to such accounts include both the preset employer contributions, as well as any contributions coming from an employee. On top of this, earnings on investments are also accrued in defined contribution plan accounts.

With defined contribution plans, solely the contributions from employers are pledged to the accounts. Future benefits are not assured. In such plans, the benefits in the future go up and down based on the results of earnings on investments held in the plans.

Savings and thrift plans prove to be the most generally seen type of defined contribution plans. With this kind of a plan, employees put in to the account a pre arranged percentage of their typically pre taxed earnings. The monies go to the employee's individual account. Part of the contributions, or all of them in some cases, are then matched up by the employee's employer.

Once these pre set contributions are credited to the individual employees' accounts from both employees and employers, these contributions are subsequently invested. They might be invested in to the stock market, for example. The resulting investment returns are finally appointed to the account on an individual basis. This is the case whether the returns prove to be positive or negative.

When retirement time arrives for an employee, the participant's account then pays out benefits for retirement. This can occur through the account buying an annuity that will then assure a regular stream of income. In recent years, these defined contribution plans have expanded to be found in nearly all countries. For numerous nations, these are currently the main type of plan for the private sector retirement schemes. This growth in defined contribution plans has occurred at the expense of defined benefit plans, also known as pension plans, as employers seek to avoid the considerable expenses in funding and maintaining pension plans.

Money that is put into these defined contribution plans may come from employer contributions or salary deferral of an employee. These plans over time have evolved to become fairly easily portable from one job and company to the next as an employee changes companies. This did not always turn out to be the case.

One unique feature of defined contribution plans revolve around the rewards and risks of investments undertaken. Every employee is responsible for his or her own account's performance, rather than the employer or sponsor of the plan. Besides this, employees are not made to buy annuities with the retirement savings. This means that they could theoretically live beyond their retirement assets, and they take on the risk of this possibility. In Great Britain, the law requires that the majority of the retirement funds be employed in buying an annuity so that this does not happen.

Delinquency

Delinquency refers to primarily an individual (but also conceivably an entity or business) failing to make good on what was expected of them according to their duty or the law. It often pertains to failing to affect the minimum due payment or carry out a fiduciary responsibility. An individual who practices Delinquency is called a delinquent. These persons have contractually undertaken obligations to turn in payments on loan accounts according to a pre-arranged routine deadline.

This might include minimum monthly amounts of money owed on a car payment, a credit card payment, or a mortgage payment. As the individuals do not make these payments on time, they become delinquent. When mortgage holders become delinquent, the financial institutions holding the loans are able to start working through foreclosure processes. They will do this when the mortgage account stays unpaid for a specific length of time.

There are many different types of accounts on which people fall into Delinquency. This could be retail account payments, income taxes, mortgages, lines of credit, and more. Individuals who become delinquent suffer the consequences for these financial actions. Such impacts vary with the kind of Delinquency, cause, and length of time it has continued in this unfortunate state. As individuals become late on credit card bills, they can be charged late fees. Those who do not make their required tax payments can have their wages garnered or even their bank account levied by the Internal Revenue Service.

Besides these financial Delinquencies, there are responsibilities which when they are not carried out can be labeled delinquent. By not carrying out one's fiduciary duties, professional responsibilities, or other contractual obligations as set forth by custom or the law, individuals can be called delinquents as well. Police officers who do not professionally carry out their responsibilities to protect ordinary citizens in the line of duty can be found to be delinquent.

It is important not to confuse Delinquency with default. Individuals are officially delinquent at the point when they miss making a required payment of some sort in a timely fashion. By contrast, loan defaults happen as borrowers do not pay back a loan according to the terms on which they agreed to in their original contract. Loans can stay in the delinquent stage without being treated as in default for an unspecified amount of time. The amount of time this remains delinquent rather than in default varies considerably from one creditor and financial institution to another. For example, with student loans, the United States' Federal Government permits these to be fully delinquent for as long as 270 consecutive days before they become considered to be in default.

The U.S. keeps track of its various national Delinquency rates. Per the year 2016 in the fourth quarter, such Delinquencies amounted to 4.15 percent for real estate loans on residential loans, 2.15 percent on loans for consumer credit cards, and .85 percent for real estate loans on commercial loans. The government also maintains official statistics for these rates by year of loan issued. For 2016, this amounted to 2.04 percent, which was near the historically typical average.

The devastating global financial crisis and U.S. mortgage crisis which erupted in 2007 caused the rates to spike to a high in the Great Recession years which reached fully 7.4 percent in the year 2010 in its first quarter. For residential real estate, the rate topped out at 11.26 percent for these specific types of loans. Up to the year 2008 in its second quarter these Delinquencies had not been higher than three percent all the way back to the year 1994 in its first quarter.

Delinquent Rent

Delinquent Rent refers to rent that tenants pay their landlords late. This is called one of the two greatest frustrations for landlords in the renting process. The other one is handling tenants who vandalize a place. Making good on late or unpaid rent is a hassle for landlords that is almost always an expensive and time consuming process. There are various processes available to landlords for them to obtain their unpaid or late rents. These vary widely based on the state where the property lies, as each state has its own laws pertaining to rentals. The rental agreement also plays its part based on the provisions it contains.

Rental relationships were once arranged with mere handshakes, but that simpler time is now long gone forever. In today's complicated and litigious world, such business arrangements become specified by the law and in contracts instead of on a trust basis. In today's rental arrangements, the rental agreement governs the means of obtaining Delinquent Rent or unpaid balances. This is why it is so important to obtain a solid rent contract template before individuals become landlords and execute rental agreements for the first time.

Oral arrangements are never a good idea in these scenarios. This is because courts frown on enforcing them and they may even doubt their existence or validity. Well-defined lease contracts spell out each provision of the rental arrangements. This includes the amount of rent that has to be furnished and at what point said rent must be paid. Landlords who are unable to specify the precise date on which the rent must be paid will find they are often stymied in their subsequent late and unpaid rent collection endeavors.

It is similarly important for landlords to never agree to verbal alterations to a written out and executed contract. Verbal changes become hotly contested and debatable in law courts. They often will diminish the ability to collect on late rents which the written contract adequately specified. This is why instead the landlords must focus on writing in the maximum number of self help (for rental collection) avenues as the laws in a given state will permit.

In the majority of cases, the state laws provide for two different forms of dealing with unpaid and Delinquent Rent. The ones mentioned above are called self help remedies. These involve any methods a landlord may enforce without needing to make court appearances, file lawsuits, and involve judges. They can only include the relevant property code and state rental law provision allowances. Some of these so-called self help remedies include the ability to enforce liens on the personal property of the renter, to post a notice of eviction, and to physically engage in a lockout of the tenant by changing the locks on the property.

There are states that restrict the kinds of personal property that landlords may seize against Delinquent Rent or back rent. State contract law usually has provisions governing lockouts and eviction notices too. Landlords have to obey the contractual and state law requirements for both methods carefully. For example, shutting off electricity, water, and gas is typically not permitted by most states among the procedures for collecting late rent.

Eviction notices are often the most effective means of dealing with back rent. This is because the majority of tenants do not actually wish to be evicted forcefully by the sheriff from the property. The will generally respond to such a notice by paying any and all rent which they owe at this point.

When self help remedies do not resolve the situation, the small claims court is the place that handles the majority of landlord-tenant disputes. The landlord will have to pay filing fees in order to lodge a rent collection lawsuit. Tenants must be notified of the opening of such a rental dispute lawsuit. Every jurisdiction has its own regulations for the format of the notice which the landlord must provide to the tenant. Among these are in person notification, by fax, by mail, or other means of notification. Once a hearing is held before the judge, a judgment will typically be awarded for the rent that remains unpaid or delinquent.

Depreciation

Depreciation is the means of spreading out the price of a usable physical asset during the period of its practical life. Businesses engage in this process of depreciating assets for accounting and taxing purposes. Depreciation can also be the reduction of the value of an asset that poor market conditions create.

Where accounting and taxing purposes are concerned, the process of depreciation demonstrates the portion of the value of the asset in question that has been utilized. Where taxes are concerned, the rules are stricter. The IRS sets out the regulations for taking depreciation of tangible assets.

Businesses are permitted to deduct the expenses of the asset they buy as a business expense. They simply must abide by the IRS' rules as far as when and how much of the deduction they are permitted to log. This all comes down to which category the asset falls in and the amount of time for which it is expected to last.

In accounting, businesses attempt to correlate the cost of a particular asset with the amount of income that it practically earns the company. With regards to an item of equipment that costs them $1 million, it may have a practical life expectancy of 10 years. They would depreciate this asset over the course of ten years. The company would then expense out $100,000 of the asset value each accounting year. They would match up the income that the equipment generated the company every year as well.

Accountants can use depreciation tricks to impact the company's financial bottom line. This is because with enough depreciation, the income statement, cash flow statement, balance sheet, and statement of the owners' equity will all be impacted significantly. It is true that certain depreciation assumptions can have significant impacts on both the long term asset values and the results of short term earnings.

Other assets can see their value depreciated by unfortunate circumstances or poor conditions in the market. Two standout examples of this type include real estate and currencies. In the housing crisis of 2008, many home owners living in the most severely impacted markets like Las Vegas watched helplessly as their home values depreciated by even 50% of the value. The post Brexit vote results day saw the British pound plunge by over 10% in a single day.

Generally accepted accounting principles affect depreciation figures. This is because a company might pay for a long life asset in cash, as with a tractor trailer that delivers its goods to customers. According to GAAP principles though, this expense would not be shown as a cost against income then and there. Rather than this, the expense is listed as an asset on the company balance sheet. The value of the asset is consistently and continuously reduced out during the in-service life of the asset in question. As the expense is reduced, this is a form of depreciating the asset.

This is done because GAAP principles insist that all expenses must be recorded along with the accounting time-frame as are the revenues which they generate. In the example of the tractor trailer that costs $100,000 and lasts for approximately ten years, GAAP would look to see what the salvage value would be at the end of that time. Assuming it expected the trailer to be worth $10,000 at the end of the depreciating period, than the expense would be depreciated at a rate of $9,000 for each of the ten years (using the formula of cost – salvage value/number of years depreciating).

With long term assets, the depreciating typically involves two lines. There would commonly be one that displayed the price of the assets and another that demonstrated the amount of depreciating that had been charged off against the assets' value.

Depression

Depressions in economics are loosely defined as major declines in a country's GDP, or gross domestic product. The gross domestic product is made up of four major components. These include money that consumers spend, government spending for goods and labor, investment affected by government agencies and individual companies, and the net sum of the country's exported products.

All of these elements are combined to come up with the country's annual gross domestic product. Another simpler way of stating the GDP is in the counting of everything spent on services, goods, research, investments, and labor in the nation.

Depressions are then commonly said to happen as the country's GDP drops by minimally ten percent in only a year. There is not any consensus on the precise amount of decline in terms of percentage that must occur. Following the notorious stock market crash in 1929, the Great Depression that happened in the United States and throughout Europe demonstrated a sharp decline in GDP not only the first year but also over the following years.

In the months that came after this market crash, the U.S. GDP fell by in excess of thirty percent. After that it rose for a while, though not nearly to the pre-crash levels seen earlier in the U.S. This demonstrates the difficulty in simply defining depressions simply by looking at GDP declines and increases.

The Great Depression is mostly held to have continued until the very end of the 1930's decade. Real recovery nationally then did not begin until the outbreak of World War II in 1939. The reason that this is the case is that additional factors besides simply GDP declines have to be considered in evaluating what is and is not truly a depression.

The Great Depression had many negative characteristics besides simply falling GDP's. With plummeting industrial output, major numbers of jobs disappeared. As significantly smaller amounts of money came into workers hands, a great deal less could be spent on consumer goods or business investments. Without this money circulating back to businesses, firms were unable to hire workers back. The numbers of people dependent on help from the public assistance funds were greater. Job recovery did not materialize as hoped.

From time to time the Gross Domestic Product did rise in the 1930's. It never returned to the normalcy seen before the beginning of the Great Depression until the United States became fully involved in the Second World War. Demands for military equipment and weapons for the war did many things to help the American economy. Young men found employment in the army, industry suddenly had rising demand for military products, and job openings were more than the able bodied people available to fill them. At this point, women began entering jobs in industry in the place of men for the first time.

Nowadays, some respected economists worry that a depression like one not seen since the thirties could again be gripping the nation. This is because unemployment from the Great Recession remains stubbornly high, goods and services' prices are rising at a faster pace than payrolls in the majority of industries, and requirements for public assistance are higher than they have been since the end of the Second World War. The biggest fear today is that many of the jobs that are disappearing, such as technology and manufacturing, will never return, as they are migrating overseas to countries where workers are paid significantly less.

Digital Currency

A digital currency refers to an asset which possesses numerous interesting and groundbreaking characteristics. On the one hand, they are much like traditional forms of money that people spend and keep, such as cash and coins. On the other hand, such currencies are not physical. This means that they do not have literal physical representations or the associated physical limitations. This currency is kept in a digital wallet, which can have physical characteristics if it is a cold storage type of digital wallet.

Digital currency in particular and electronic money in general is gradually becoming more significant as the world continuously evolves into a society that is more and more cashless. The amount of money supply which is expressed in digital format is constantly growing. Thanks to the rising popularity of such crypto-currencies as especially Bitcoin, there now exists the distinct possibility of migrating entirely away from traditional paper bills and coins at some point in the future.

Such digital currency only can exist and function when secure transactions are guaranteed online. This makes these currencies both an occupant and hostage of digital environments. They are generally represented and depicted in the form of information. Bitcoin has become so popular that numerous companies currently accept this form of digital currency. PayPal even allows for the utilization of Bitcoin now.

It is interesting to note that Bitcoin is not the only digital currency option available to individuals and businesses for transactions. A range of such currencies exist which can be used to pay for transactions. The next five most important after Bitcoin are Litecoin, Darkcoin, Peercoin, Dogecoin, and Primecoin. They have many advantages over traditional money.

The first of these is the instant transfer ability. Individuals are no longer required to wait on a central clearinghouse somewhere to handle the transaction. The days of from one to five business days waits for transfers are long gone thanks to these digital currencies. Crypto-currencies are so popular precisely because the effect of such a transfer is instantaneous.

The majority of these digital currencies also come with no fees. Whatever something costs in Bitcoin or another such digital currency, people simply pay with it at transaction cost and no hidden fees are applied. This is a stark difference from many credit card or even PayPal transactions.

Individuals and businesses especially love the fact that these digital currencies come completely without borders. This means that a seller or buyer does not have to be concerned with exchange rates or foreign transaction fees (which are often exorbitant). Cross border transactions are simple and effective to put through, though people must still watch the exchange rate at which they are offered in the local currency into which they are paying.

For the majority of applications and scenarios, these crypto-currencies also prove to be extremely secure. It is the digital wallet where the danger lies. The money is not being stored in a bank vault or even on a bank computer. The wallet must be backed up on a daily basis to prevent it from being lost. In order to ensure that it is secure, the only way to guarantee this is by utilizing cold storage.

Cold storage takes the digital wallet completely offline and off network. It means that the "pin code" like authorization element will be stored on a small device that resembles a USB miniature drive device. The nature of these devices is that they do not accept software. This means that Trojan Horses and viruses which steal information can not be imprinted on them. They also are never online long enough to be hacked, as users only connect them to a computer long enough to digitally sign the transaction.

These digital currencies have convincingly changed the rules of the financial transaction game. Their limits are two fold. The first is that a business must be willing to accept Bitcoin or rival currencies in order for a consumer to pay with it. The second is that digital currency regulation is inevitable. Central banks are jealous animals. They are already suspicious of their monopolized currency-printing functions being assumed in a non-regulated and more difficult to track environment by a non-centralized form of money.

Digital Wallet

A digital wallet is an electronic type of device which makes it possible for individuals to complete financial transactions electronically. They are also called e-wallets. There are several useful applications for using this technology. Consumers can utilize them to buy thing over the Internet with a computer or laptop. They might also employ them to buy an item or service in a store by using their smart phone to complete the transaction. These electronic wallets can be linked up directly to the person's bank account as well.

These phone versions of digital wallets could also contain a health card, driver's license, loyalty memberships, and similar important identification documents. The technology permits these credentials to be transferred over to the terminal of the merchant wirelessly. The technology specifically is called NFC near field communication. More and more these days, these electronic wallets are being deployed to do more than conclude simple financial transactions. They also can verify the characteristics of the holder.

As an example, a digital wallet can be used to verify the buyer's age in the store when they are there buying alcohol or cigarettes. In Japan, such systems have become increasingly more popular. People there call the electronic wallets "wallet mobiles."

Another advantage to such digital wallets concerns their ability to remember more complicated passwords. The owners do not have to be worried about if they will be personally capable of remembering them when they need them. These wallets also have the advantage of cutting the need to have a physical wallet with them. Consumer data centers and companies love them because they make it easy for them to gather consumer data. Such information helps them to better understand the purchasing habits of customers. This makes it easier to appropriately market goods and services to them. Naturally consumers suffer a great breach of their privacy thanks to these e-wallets and the resulting consumer data collection practices.

The advantage for consumers is that these e-wallets can save them having to fill in various order forms on different websites whenever they perform an online purchase. This is because that data is pre-stored on the wallet and auto entered (and updated) to the appropriate order fields on all merchant sites thanks to the technology of the digital wallet. Statistics shows that individuals will abandon online purchases fully 25 percent of the time because they become frustrated in filling out the forms.

Both consumers and merchants each obtain advantages thanks to these e-wallets. Consumers gain the significant advantage of having all of their sensitive information electronically encrypted. This means that it is effectively protected utilizing a secret proprietary software code. Merchants obtain the advantage of gaining safety from fraud.

Two great advantages to these digital wallets are that they are free for individuals and they are not difficult to get. Examples of this ease in obtaining them abound. Customers can complete a purchase on the site of a merchant that is developed to process server side e-wallets. All the customers have to do is to type in their names, shipping address, and payment information directly to the form provided by the merchant. When the purchase is complete, the consumer has the choice to sign on to an e-wallet which they select by simply typing in a password and user name for any future needs and purchases. Users can also obtain such a wallet at the vending web site for e-wallets.

These wallets may be free for individuals to use, but the vendors make their money off of the merchants. There are vendors of these wallets which arrange deals with the various merchants to give the wallet vendor a certain set percentage on each purchase amount which runs through their wallets. There are other cases where the e-wallet vendors run the transactions between merchants who participate and cardholders. They do this in exchange for a flat fee.

Discover

Discover Financial Services turns out to be a United States' based global financial service outfit. They issue and service the Discover Card and Diners Club International Card and operate Pulse Networks. Their flagship card proves to be the third biggest brand of credit cards within the U.S. based on the number of cards in use. The company boasts almost 50 million different card holders nationally.

Sears began the Discover legacy by introducing the card originally back in 1985. It launched the original credit card with cash rewards a year later in 1986. Stock broker Dean Witter acquired the card from Sears and then later merged its company with Morgan Stanley in 1997. The Discover Financial Services first acquired its independence with the spin off of the company in 2007. It became a publicly traded corporation headquartered in Riverwoods, Illinois, a Chicago suburb.

The company is involved with both credit cards and banking. This business offers their proprietary brand credit cards, personal loans, private student loans, checking and savings accounts, home equity loans, money market accounts, and certificates of deposit to its clients.

Their customers include both consumers and small businesses today who utilize their travel, cash, and gift cards throughout the U.S. and the world. Their two banking affiliates are Bank of New Castle and Discover Bank. Both are regulated and chartered through the FDIC and the Office of the Delaware State Bank Commissioner. The FDIC is both their insurer and federal regulator.

Besides being among the largest credit card issuers in the country and a significant bank, the company also owns and operates the PULSE network. This is a national leading network of ATM/debit machines. For more than three decades they have provided this among the largest in the country networks.

It offers services to over 4,500 credit unions, banks, and other financial institutions throughout the United States. Cardholders are linked up with POS payment terminals and ATM machines around the U.S. through their services. PULSE is technologically advanced in its offering of simultaneous transaction processing and settlement.

They also own Diners Club International since 2008. This globally known brand provides financial payment services and credit for small businesses, corporations, and consumers. Launched in 1950, Diners Club International provided the world's original multiple use credit cards. Its cards boast acceptance in over 185 countries via millions of cash access points and merchant locations across the globe today.

Thanks to these combined operations, literally billions of different financial transactions go through their network of electronic payments every year. The Discover Network handles a complete line up of cards, including prepaid, debit, and credit cards. Their programs and tools were created to assist merchants, acquirers, and issues in growing their transactional volumes and operating their payment processing needs with effective and efficient operations. Internationally, the network relies on two different alliances that help to ensure the card is well accepted overseas. China UnionPay and JCB offer and receive reciprocal card acceptance throughout numerous nations around the globe.

Discover prides itself on its long running customer satisfaction success. For three years in a row through 2016, it has been ranked the "Highest in Customer Satisfaction with Credit Card Companies" by J.D. Power.

Diversifying

Diversifying refers to the means of effectively lowering your investing risk by putting your money into a wide range of various assets. A truly well diversified portfolio offers the benefits of lower amounts of risk than those that are simply invested into one or two asset classes or kinds of investments.

Everyone should engage in some amount of diversification, even if the individual proves to be one who is tolerant of risk. Those individuals who really fear the present day economic uncertainties and very real amounts of risk in the market place will perform better forms of diversification into more asset groups.

Mainstream diversification is always recommended by financial experts because of the common example of not placing all of your investment eggs into just a single basket. If you do have all eggs in the one basket and then drop the basket along the way, then they can all break. The idea is that by placing each egg into its own individual basket, the odds of breaking all of the eggs declines significantly, even if one or several of them do get broken themselves.

Portfolios that have not engaged in diversifying might have only one or two corporations' stocks in them. This proves to be a dangerous investment strategy, since no matter how good a company looks on paper, its stock could decline to as low as zero literally over night. The past few years of the financial collapse have taught many investors the extremely painful lesson that even once blue chip financial companies' stock can decline to practically nothing as they spectacularly collapse.

Any financial expert will confidently state that portfolios made up of a dozen or two dozen varying stocks will have far less chance of plummeting. This becomes even more the case when you pick out stocks from a variety of types, industries, and market capitalization sizes of corporations. Better diversifying in stocks would include some companies that are based in other countries. Diversifying does not simply stop with stocks. It steers investors into bonds, mutual funds, and money market funds as well. Though all of these different investments diversify you, they still leave you mostly exposed to the one currency of the U.S. dollar.

More thorough diversifying will put at least a portion of your investments into assets whose values are not solely expressed in terms of only the American currency. This would include commodities, such as gold, silver, oil, and platinum in particular. Foreign currencies, such as the Euro, Pound, or Swiss Franc are another fantastic means of diversifying, and they can be acquired on the world FOREX exchange in currency accounts.

Real estate, including commercial properties, residential properties, vacation homes, or even real estate investment funds, offers another way to diversify away from U.S. dollar based financial investments such as stocks, bonds, mutual funds, and money market accounts. The strongest diversifying advice is to have at least three to seven completely different investment class vehicles, preferably one or more of which is not denominated in only U.S. dollars.

Dividend

Dividends represent portions of a company's earnings that are returned to the investors in the company's stock. These are typically paid out in cash that is either deposited into the investors' brokerage accounts or can be reinvested directly into the company's stock. As an example of a dividend, every share of Phillip Morris pays around 4.5% dividends on the stock price each year.

Investing in dividend paying stocks is a particular passive income investment strategy that is also a cash flow investment. This passive, or cash flow, income means that you collect income just from holding these stock investments. This kind of strategy entails building up a group of blue chip company stocks that pay large dividend yields which add money to your account usually four times per year, on a quarterly basis. Investors in dividends tremendously enjoy watching these routine deposits in cash arrive in either their bank account, brokerage account, or the mail.

Dividend investors who understand this type of investment are looking for a number of different elements in the stocks that they buy. Such dividend stocks should include a high dividend yield. To qualify as high yields, most value investors prefer to see ones that pay more than do the interest rate yields on U.S. Treasuries. Dividend yields can be easily determined. All that you have to do is to take the amount of the dividend and divide it by the price of the stock. So a stock that offers a $2 dividend and costs $40 is paying a five percent dividend yield.

Dividend paying stocks should also feature high dividend coverage. This coverage simply refers to the safety of a dividend, or how likely it is to be reduced or even eliminated. Companies that earn their profits from a large array of businesses are more likely to be able to continue paying their dividends than are companies that make all of their money off of a single business that could be threatened.

A more tangible way of expressing the coverage lies in how many times the dividend total dollar amount is covered by the corporation's total earnings. A company with fifty million dollars in profits that pays twenty million in dividends has its dividend covered by two and a half times. Should their profits drop by ten percent or more, they will have no trouble still paying the same dividend amount to shareholders. The dividend payout ratio is another way of measuring this. On the above example it would be forty percent. Dividend investors prefer to see no more than sixty percent of profits given out as dividends, as this could signify that the company lacks future opportunities for growth and expansion.

Qualified dividends are a third element that dividend investors are looking for in their dividend paying stocks. This simply means that stocks that are kept for less than a year do not benefit from lower tax rates on dividends. Since the government is attempting to convince you to become a longer term investor, you should take advantage of these lower tax rates by only buying stocks with qualified dividends that you have held for a full year and more.

Dividend Stocks

Dividend Stocks refer to stocks that pay especially generous and predictable shares of the corporate earnings out to their share holders. They are especially important for those investors who require dependable continuous streams of income off of their investment portfolios, such as retirees. This is why the optimal stock portfolio for those who are officially retired includes a strong and diverse mixture of industry-leading corporations which provide consistent, generous dividend yields.

These Dividend Stocks are famous for paying out significant stock dividends as a distribution on their earnings. They may pay this in the form of additional shares or as cash, depending on the wishes of the share holder in question. Sometimes the company will declare a stock dividend instead of a cash dividend, removing the ability of the shareholder to choose the form in which the dividend actually pays. When dividends become payable strictly as more stock, they are also known as stock splits.

For the companies that declare regular cash dividends of these Dividend Stocks, with each share stake holders have, they receive a set portion of the earnings from the corporation. This is literally being paid for simply owning the stock shares.

Consider a real world example to better understand how these Dividend Stocks work out in practice. Gillette, the world famous market leader in the shaving razors industry, may pay a dividend of $4 on an annual basis. Typically these dividends will be paid practically on a quarterly basis. This means four times each year Gillette would provide a $1 payout for each share of stock which the stake holders possess. If an investor owned 100 shares, he or she would receive four checks per year of $100 each check at approximately the conclusion of each quarter.

Most dividends from these Dividend Stocks come out in cash. Investors have the option to have them reinvested into additional company stock shares. Sometimes the corporation will provide a more advantageous reinvestment price than the current market prices to encourage such reinvesting of dividends in the company stock. These plans are called DRIPS (Dividend Re Investment Plans).

There are also occasional special dividends offered on an only one-time basis. They could be provided if the company wins a large and lucrative lawsuit, liquidates its share of an investment and receives a windfall payout, or sells part of the business to another firm for cash. These dividends can be made in cash, property, or stock share dividends.

There are several important dates with which Dividend Stocks' investors need to be familiar. These are declaration date, date of record, ex-dividend date, and payment date. Declaration date is the calendar day when the company's Board of Directors announces a dividend payout. This is the point where the firm adds a liability for the dividend payout to its company books. This means that it owes money (or shares) to the stake holders. This date will be the one when they announce both the date of record as well as the dividend payment date.

The date of record is the one where the corporation will review the appropriate records to determine who is holding the shares and is thus eligible for the dividends. Only holders of record will receive the dividend payment. The ex-dividend date is the day after which any investors who wish to receive dividends must own the shares. Only stake holders who possess shares on the day before the ex-dividend date get paid. Finally dividends are literally doled out on the payment date.

While most stock companies will pay out dividends on either a quarterly or half yearly basis, real estate investment trusts are structured differently. They pay out their dividends on an every-month basis as they receive monthly income from their various commercial, industrial, and/or residential properties.

Down Payment

A down payment is an upfront amount that is given as a portion of the price on a purchase of large ticket items such as houses or cars. These are given in cash or by check when the contract is signed. The balance of the sum due is then given as a loan.

Down payments are principally intended to make sure that the bank or other type of lending institution is capable of recovering the remaining balance that is owed on a loan should the borrower choose to default. In transactions of real estate, the underlying asset becomes collateral that secures the associated loan against potential default.

Should the borrower not repay the loan as agreed, then the bank or institutional lender is allowed to sell this collateral asset and keep enough of the money received to pay off the rest of the loan along with the interest and fees included. In these cases, down payments decrease the exposure risk of the lender to an amount that is smaller than the collateral's value. This increases the chance of the bank getting the entire principal loaned out back should the borrower default.

The amount of such a down payment therefore impacts the lender's exposure to the loan and protects against anything that might lessen the collateral's value. This includes profits that are lost from the point of the final payment to the final collateral sale. The making of this down payment assures a lender that the borrower has capital available for long term investments, further proof that the finances of the borrower are able to afford the item in the first place. Should a borrower not successfully pay down the full loan amount, then he or she will lose the entire down payment.

Down payments on houses bought in the United States typically range anywhere from 3.5% to 20% of the full purchase amount. The Federal Housing Administration helps first time borrowers to pay merely 3.5% as a down payment. In the excesses of the years leading up to the financial collapse of 2007, many banks were making loans with no down payments. On car purchases, these amounts of down payments might be in the range of from 3% to 13%.

Electronic Funds Transfer (EFT)

EFT is the usual acronym for Electronic Funds Transfer. This program refers to the all-electronic money transfer processed out of one bank account and into another. This could be done within a single bank or over a number of different and often intermediary financial institutions. Computer systems handle these transactions entirely unaided by the intervention of human bank personnel. There are actually many different names for EFTs. Within the United States, they are often called e-checks or even electronic checks.

The phrase relates to a wide range of varying payment systems. Some of these are bank debit card or other credit card payments which a cardholding customer initiates voluntarily at a store or merchant, direct debit payments in which the firm directly debits the bank account of the consuming customers in payment for their services or goods, and payer initiated direct deposit. Other examples of this EFTs include wire transfers done utilizing the SWIFT banking international network, private currency transactions that deal with electronic money storage, and online banking electronic bill pay services that are often delivered via Electronic Funds Transfer or alternatively by using paper based checks.

Government agencies within the United States have also taken to utilizing Electronic Funds Transfers in recent years. The federal government touts them as an efficient and often practical means of collecting money and similarly paying it out electronically without having to engage in the time consuming and wasteful process of resorting to relying on paper based checks, purchasing and obtaining stamps, and generally considerable processing and mailing time lags. They encourage government agencies to adopt this payment technology if they have not already.

As the Federal Government has recently noted, EFT payments are secure, safe, and efficient. They are also less costly to utilize than any form of paper check collection or payment process. As a clear and concrete example, it helps to consider a real world case. The federal government calculates that it requires a full $1.03 in order to make a payment via a check. This represents over a dollar for a single payment transaction. Naturally this cost adds up considerably when agencies are engaging in millions of individual payments per month. Compare these costs with the government expenses for running payments via electronic formats. Every time the government enters and initiates an electronic funds transfer, it only pays the equivalent of .105 dollars (or slightly more than a single dime) per individual transaction.

In order to participate in either the government's version of EFT or any bank's version of electronic funds transfer, individuals must first sign up for the payment platform. Nowadays, all federal benefits have been switched over to and must be paid out electronically, which makes this more critical and timely to do now than ever before. For any person who receives any kind of these benefits, including SSI Supplemental Security Income, Social Security payments, civil service retirement payments, Veteran's benefits, railroad retirement payments, or military federal retirement, all benefits must be received by electronic funds transfer in order to be processed and paid out each month.

There are still other benefits which both the federal government and other private parties pay utilizing Electronic Funds Transfers. The Federal government calls its various benefit payment programs either Direct Express or Go Direct. Private parties and banks utilize a range of different labels and names for these various privately run programs.

Employee Stock Option (ESO)

Employee stock options are call options that are awarded privately rather than publicly. They turn out to be the most common form of equity compensation provided to employees of a business. Companies give out these options to their employees to provide them with an incentive to build up the market value of the company. These options may not be sold on the open markets.

An ESO provides the receiving employees with the right but not obligation to buy a preset quantity of shares of the company. The contract specifies a time frame within which these must be acquired before they expire worthless. The price they employees can buy them at is the current price which becomes the strike price. These time limits for using them are generally ten years. Companies spell all of these terms out in the options agreement.

These options are only valuable to the employee if the price of the company stock increases during the exercise time-frame. This is because the employees then are able to purchase the discounted shares at the same time as they sell them for the greater price on the market. The difference between the two prices represents their profit.

If the share price of the company declines, they are unable to use them and will see them eventually expire worthless. This is why companies utilize employee stock options instead of large salaries to encourage their employees. This provides the companies with great incentive to build up the value of the company. Three principle types of ESO exist in the form of non statutory, incentive, and reload employee stock options.

Non statutory employee stock options are also called non-qualified. These prove to be the normal kinds of ESOs. In such a contract, employees are not permitted to use these options during the vesting period. This vesting timeframe ranges from one to three years. When they are sold, the employee makes the spread between current price and strike price times the number of shares he or she sells. These types of ESOs become taxable at the employee's regular income tax level.

Graduated vesting in these options allows the employees to sell a percentage of the options such as maybe 10% in the first year. Each year another 10% would become available until the full 100% level is achieved by year ten. Incentive stock options are set up to lower taxes as much as possible. Employees can not exercise the option to buy the stock until after a year. They can not actually sell the stock until another year after buying it.

This type of option creates a risk that the stock price may decline over the year long holding time frame. The advantage to the employee is that these ISOs receive far better tax treatment. The tax rate defaults to the long term capital gains rate instead of the traditional full income tax rate. Upper level management are usually the ones who receive such tax advantageous ISOs from their companies.

The third type of employee stock options are called Reload ESOs. These begin their contract lives as non-statutory ESOs. The employees engage in their first exercise of the contract where they make money on the transaction. At this point, the employees who exercise are given a special reload of the employee stock option. In this process the company issues new options to the employee. The present market price at time of issue becomes the new strike price for the reloaded options. This way the employee is constantly re-incentivized to perform for the company.

Equifax

Equifax today is an agency that reports consumer credit within the U.S. Analysts number it among the big three American credit bureau agencies alongside rivals Trans Union and Experian. The company proves to be the oldest of the three main credit bureaus in the country as it became established back in 1899.

The firm gathers and keeps information on more than 800 million consumers and over 88 million businesses around the globe. They are headquartered in Atlanta, Georgia and remain a worldwide data services provider that has annual revenues of $2.7 billion. They have over 7,000 staff operating in 14 different countries. The company is listed on the NYSE New York Stock Exchange. One of their many divisions (Equifax Workforce Solutions) is among the 55 national contractors which the United States Department of Health and Human Services hired to help develop the federal government's HealthCare.gov website.

The original company which later became Equifax was Retail Credit Company founded in 1899. The firm rapidly expanded and already counted offices around both the United States and Canada by 1920. In the 1960s, this Retail Credit Company represented among the largest of the credit bureaus. It contained files for millions of American and Canadian citizens.

While the firm engaged in some credit reporting at the time, the main part of their business came from providing reports to the many insurance companies throughout the U.S. and Canada as consumers applied for insurance policies such as auto, life, medical, and fire insurance lines. Back in the day, every one of the significant insurance firms relied on Retail Credit Company to gather their information on health, morals, habits, finances, and the utilization of cars and vehicles. Besides this, the firm investigated various insurance claims and also gave employment reports out to companies as consumers sought new jobs. The majority of their credit reporting work at that time they delegated to a subsidiary company called Retailers Commercial Agency.

In 1975, the company changed its name to be Equifax because of image problems they had earned by keeping shady and intimate personal details on all American's lives and selling them to anyone willing to pay. It was after this that the new company Equifax expanded its operations into commercial credit reporting on firms located in the United States, the United Kingdom, and Canada. Here it engaged in competition against such firms as Experian and Dun & Bradstreet. In the 1990s, they began to phase out their insurance reporting operations and spun off their division which gathered and sold specialist credit information to insurance companies. Among this was the CLUE Comprehensive Loss Underwriting Exchange database they had developed, which they included in the Choice Point spinoff back in 1997.

Throughout the vast majority of its company history, the firm engaged mostly in the B2B sector. They sold insurance and consumer credit reports and associated analytics to businesses which operated in a variety of industries and segments. Among these were insurance firms, retailers, utilities, healthcare providers, banks, credit unions, government agencies, specialty finance companies, personal finance operations, and various other kinds of financial institutions.

Since they divested from their insurance reporting primary operation, the company sells information which includes business credit and consumer credit reports, demographic information, analytics, and software. Their credit reports offer a wide and detailed profile on the payment history and personal creditworthiness of individuals and businesses. This reveals how well these groups have honored their various financial obligations, including paying back loans and bills.

Starting in 1999, Equifax started offering its vast services into the consumer credit sector. They also began consumer operations with such important services as protection from identity theft and from credit fraud. The company along with its other two main rivals is required to offer American residents a single free credit file report once per year. The data from the U.S. Equifax credit records becomes incorporated into the Annual Credit Report.com website.

Equity

Equity represents the homeowner's total dollar amount of ownership in their property. Determining equity is a simple calculation. It is found by taking the home's assumed fair market value and subtracting out the balances of liens and debts secured by the property along with the mortgage balance that is still unpaid. As a home owner pays down the mortgage, reducing the outstanding principal balance, the equity of a home owner goes up. It similarly increases as the property gains in value. To obtain one hundred percent equity in their property, home owners have to pay down both any outstanding debts that are secured by the property and the full mortgage.

Associated with the equity value of a home is the LTV, or loan to value ratio. This loan to value ratio proves to be a means of stating the property's value as against the total dollar amount of your actual loan. The loan to value ratio is simply figured up by taking the amount of your loan and dividing it by your property value. Alternatively, you could divide the amount of your loan by the purchase price or selling price, whichever of the two is the lower amount.

An example helps to illustrate the concept. If you were to purchase a $300,000 house, you might put down a $60,000 down payment using your money. The remaining $240,000 would be covered by taking out a mortgage. Dividing the $60,000 amount by the $300,000 home value yields equity of twenty percent. If you divide the $240,000 by the $300,000 home value, then you will get the loan to value ratio that amounts to eighty percent.

Should you determine later that you will sell this house, then the equity that you have will be concretely and accurately figured up for you. This will simply prove to be the fair market value of your house minus the loan that you still owe the bank on the house. Using the example from the paragraph above, consider what would happen if you lived in and made payments on your house for five years following the purchase.

In this time frame, your monthly mortgage payments lower the balance that remains on the loan to the tune of $10,000, diminishing it from $240,000 to

$230,000. Besides this, over those five years, your home value goes up. This allows you to realize a selling price of $330,000. Since the balance that you owed is still $230,000, then your equity is simply figured by taking the $330,000 selling price and subtracting the $230,000 from it. This leaves you with a final equity value of $100,000. Once all selling costs and realty commissions are figured up and taken out, you would be able to utilize the $100,000 equity in order to invest or to put down the down payment on the next house that you purchase.

Naturally, this home value can cut both ways. Should the value on the home drop from $300,00 to $250,000 in the time that you own it, then your remaining equity would be only $50,000, less than the original $60,000 that you put into it upfront.

ERISA

ERISA is the acronym for The Employment Retirement Income Security Act that was enacted in 1974. This ERISA legislation set up a basic level of standards for health, retirement, and various additional types of plans for welfare benefits. These include disability insurance, life insurance, and apprenticeship plans.

This Employment Retirement Income Security Act is both overseen and run by the EBSA, which turns out to be the acronym for Employee Benefits Security Administration. This EBSA operates as a division under the United States DOL, or Department of Labor. If you have any questions about the act, concerns that you are not being treated according to the law, or complaints regarding treatment as the ERISA laws relate to you, then you should contact your area ERISA office for help and clarification.

It is important to note that these protecting regulations mandated by ERISA only pertain to non government, private employers who choose to provide benefits plans and health insurance that is employer sponsored for their employees. ERISA does not force such employers to provide such these plans for employees. Rather, it only lays out regulations for the employee offered benefits that such employers make available. It is also significant that the rules and regulations set up by ERISA do not pertain to those benefits or insurance policies that are purchased by an individual privately.

ERISA does establish the requirements and standards for a number of different related elements. Reporting and accountability is required to be detailed and made available to the U.S. Federal government. The conduct for HMO's and other managed care, as well as for other people who have financial responsibility for the administration of the plan, is strictly regulated by the ERISA rules.

ERISA also pertains to safeguards and procedures. Written policies have to be set up to determine the way that claims have to be filed, along with the claims' appeals process in writing for any claims that are denied. ERISA further stipulates that these appeals should be decided in a reasonably timed and fair way. ERISA also proves to be a protection that insures that all plans are both offered, safeguarded, and funded in the ways that most appropriately favor the members and their best interests.

ERISA does not permit discrimination in the ways that benefits in the plan are gathered and collected for those members who are qualified. Finally, ERISA insists that a variety of disclosures be made to the participants in the plan. These include a plan summary that specifically lists out the provided benefits, the associated rules for obtaining such benefits, any limitations of the plans, and other matters including getting referrals before doctor and surgeon visits.

Escrow

Escrow is a concept that relates to a sum of money that is kept by an uninvolved third party for the two parties involved in a given transaction. In the U.S., this escrow is most commonly involved where real estate mortgages are concerned. Here is it utilized for the payment of insurance and property tax during the mortgage's life.

When you place your money into such an escrow account, an escrow agent who is a neutral third party holds it. This agent works on behalf of both the borrower and home lender. The escrow agent's job in the transaction is to act as the principal parties instruct him or her. As all transaction terms are fulfilled, the money is then released. These escrow accounts may be a part of transactions ranging from small purchases affected on online auction sites to building projects that total in the multiple millions of dollars.

Escrow is utilized in these property transactions when it is time for your mortgage to close. At this point, the borrower's lender will commonly insist that you establish an escrow account for paying for both home owner's insurance and property taxes. You are required to make a first deposit to the account. After this, you make payments into the account each month. Typically, these are simply a part of your monthly mortgage payments. When it is time for your insurance premiums and taxes to be paid, your escrow agent then releases the funds.

The concept behind this escrow is to give your lender peace of mind and protection that your insurance and taxes are both paid in a timely manner. Should you not pay your property taxes, the city might place a lien on this house, making it hard for the bank to sell it if they needed to. Similarly, if a fire burned down the house and the insurance premiums had not been paid, the bank would not have any underlying collateral for the mortgage anymore.

You the borrower also benefit from this escrow account. It allows you to stretch out your taxes and insurance costs over the course of the entire year's twelve payments. As an example, your annual property taxes might prove to be $3,000, with a yearly insurance cost of $600. This would mean that when spread out over twelve even payments, the escrow costs would amount to only $300 each month.

The nice thing about escrow accounts and payments is that they come with an included safeguard built in. Should you miss a single payment, then the responsible lender is still capable of paying the accounts in a timely manner. The U.S. Federal law actually stops these lenders from storing up in excess of two months' worth of payments in escrow. As insurance and tax amounts will vary a little from one year to the next, the lender will have to examine and make adjustments to your annual escrow payments.

Eviction

Eviction involves the forced removal of a rental tenant from a landlord's rental property. Other terms that convey the same or a similar meaning include repossession, summary possession, and ejection. Eviction proves to be the term most commonly utilized in landlord and tenant communications. Evictions can not simply happen without going through a legal process that could include an eviction lawsuit.

A notice must first be given to the tenant by the landlord. This is most often referred to as the notice to vacate or notice to quit. It has to be delivered to a tenant in advance of beginning official legal eviction procedures. In most cases, the tenant will then receive somewhere from three to ten days to address the issue causing eviction. These offenses likely are caused by either a failure to pay the rent in a timely manner or contractual breach of the lease for something like have a pet.

Should the tenant refuse to leave the property in question after the expiration of the notice to quit, then the landlord next provides the tenant with a complaint. These complaints mandate that the tenant in question will have to go to court. If the tenant refuses to appear at the court date or does not provide an answer to the complaint, then the landlord is able to seek a default judgment, in which he or she automatically wins the case. A tenant response should include his or her side of the story as well as defense that could include the tenant not being provided with repairs that the lease stipulates.

Following an appropriate answer, trial dates are determined. With the issues being dependent on time, these cases are commonly hurried through the system. Should a judge back up a tenant, then the tenant is allowed to stay, although he or she would have to pay back due rent. Should the landlord be victorious, then the tenant receives a little window to move out of the property before being forcefully evicted. This is commonly only a week, though with a stay of execution, the tenant could be given more time.

Some jurisdictions permit a tenant to have a right to redemption in the eviction process. This would allow a tenant to cancel a pending eviction and to stay in the rented property by catching up immediately on the back rent along with other appropriate fees. These rights become waived should the tenant constantly be late in paying the rent.

Finally, after a tenant has lost his or her eviction lawsuit, the tenant is commonly given a particular number of days in which to abandon the property. This has to be done before other repercussions occur. Sometimes the tenant will be told to leave immediately.

Landlords are given writs of possession by the court after the tenant has lost the lawsuit and still refused to leave. These writs of possession are then turned over to a law enforcement officer. Such an officer would then put up an official notice for a tenant to depart the property before the date on which the officer will return to forcibly remove the tenant. If the tenant is not gone when the officer returns, he is permitted to take the tenant and anyone else on the property and remove them. They will be allowed to take away their possessions or place them in storage before the property is given back to the landlord.

Experian

Experian is one of the three main credit reporting bureaus in the United States. As such it maintains a credit report, history, and FICO score on all adult Americans. The company does so much more than this most commonly understood function.

The company is also an international leader for global business and consumer credit reporting as well as marketing services. Experian is headquartered in Dublin, Ireland and is based on the London Stock Exchange where it is a member of Britain's FTSE 100 stock index. The company has customers in over 80 countries of the world and maintains offices and employees in 37 countries. Besides its Dublin base, Experian has operations headquarters found in Nottingham in the United Kingdom, California in the United States, and Sao Paulo in Brazil.

Experian serves as the corporate leader in global information services. The company received the 2015 honor of "World's Most Innovative Companies" from Forbes magazine for being among the leaders in driving improvements and change.

They deliver analytical tools and data to their clients found all over the world. The company helps businesses to prevent fraud, to manage their credit risk, to automate functions of decision making, and to specifically target marketing offers.

Experian also assists individuals with information and security needs. They aid individuals in checking out their credit reports and credit scores through copies that they can purchase and download directly over the Internet. They help people to safeguard themselves against the very real dangers of identity theft with credit report monitoring services. The company also provides a great source of information for education that is both hands on and interactive. This education helps both marketing personnel and credit professionals along with individual consumers.

Experian prides itself on its analytic and data services. They are in the business of assisting businesses and individuals with managing, protecting, and optimally using their data. They offer a number of different services to help people to do this effectively.

Their Experian Credit Tracker product gives consumers their FICO score, Experian credit report, and a credit monitoring service that comes with fraud alerts. They also staff a dedicated support team for fraud resolution when individuals become victims of identity theft. Help with identity theft or credit fraud is an area that is critical to consumers when they become victims.

Consumers can also choose from their higher level Experian Protect My ID service. This gives individuals an Experian credit report, 3 bureau credit monitoring services and alerts, daily checking of ID via Internet scanning, and access to their dedicated support for fraud resolution.

Experian provides a higher level view of individuals' credit reports and scores also. Their 3 Bureau Credit Report and FICO Scores service delivers copies of the person's credit report and FICO score for Experian, TransUnion, and Equifax. They also sell just their own credit report and FICO score for a lower price.

Experian offers even more services to its big business customers. Among their business product offerings are customer acquisition, customer management, fraud management, risk management, debt recovery, consulting services, regulatory compliance, and thought leadership. In customer acquisition, the company offers direct mail tools and big data analytics.

For risk management they verify applicants' identities and backgrounds. Experian can manage data breaches and prevent money laundering as part of their fraud management offerings. Debt recovery services include locating debtors and managing collection efforts. Among their consulting services are strategy, product, and fraud consulting areas.

Small business customers also have a variety of services offered to them by Experian. These include help with business and consumer credit, marketing and managing the business, and collecting debt.

Fair Credit Billing Act

Congress passed the Fair Credit Billing act back in 1975. They enacted this national law in order to safeguard consumers from unfair or prejudiced billing actions. It created mechanisms for dealing with billing errors that affect credit accounts which are open ended. This includes credit cards and charge card accounts.

There are many different and all too common types of billing errors that the Fair Credit Billing Act specifies and protects against in its statute. Charges which are an incorrect amount are one. It also covers charges showing up on a bill that the consumer did not process. These are often known as unauthorized charges. Consumers can never be responsible for more than $50 of these. The act also covers the costs of any goods that did not come as they were supposed to when the consumer bought them, as well as for those goods that the consumer never received.

Consumers are similarly protected by the Fair Credit Billing Act from errors in calculation. They can not be held responsible for billing statements which the companies send out to the wrong address. Changes of address are required to be submitted by the account holder in writing and received by the creditor more than 19 days before the billing period ends. Consumers are similarly protected against any charges which they request proof of or clarification for on a statement. They may also not be held liable for a creditor improperly showing payments or charges to their credit accounts.

Customers are able to avail themselves of the protections spelled out in the Fair Credit Billing Act. To do so, they have to begin the process by writing the creditor at their business address specified for billing inquiries. They must include their name and address, account numbers, and any information on the billing dispute in question. The letter must be received by the creditor within 60 days or less of the original bill mailing date.

Such a letter should be dispatched by certified mail with return receipt so that the consumer has conclusive proof of when the creditor received it. All relevant copies of receipts and supporting documents need to be included with the letter. The creditor concerned is required by law to acknowledge that they have received the letter of complaint in 30 days or less after they receive it. The creditor then has up to 90 days (as in two billing cycles) to research and resolve the dispute per the terms of the Fair Credit Billing Act.

The Fair Credit Billing Act also governs what happens when a bill is placed in dispute by a consumer. The person is allowed to not make payments on any charges pertaining to the disputed amount in question. Such a period of withholding only applies throughout the time frame in which the investigation is ongoing. All remaining portions of the bill and relevant interest amounts have to be paid as per the governing credit agreement and terms. The creditor may not engage in any legal action or collection activity against the borrower so long as the investigation phase is ongoing. The account of the borrower is not permitted to be closed or restricted in this phase.

The creditor is also forbidden to make threats against the borrowers' credit ratings when charges are under investigation and in dispute. The dispute itself can be reported to the credit ratings agencies. Creditors are not allowed to discriminate by withholding credit approval from any consumer who uses his or her rights to dispute a credit charge. This means in practice that consumers may not be refused credit because they have filed disputes against charges on a bill.

Fair Housing Act

The Fair Housing Act of 1968 is officially known as Title VIII from the Civil Rights Act of 1968. It makes it illegal to discriminate with regards to renting, selling, or financing homes or apartments. No one may consider color, race, sex, religion, or national origin in these activities.

Congress amended the Fair Housing Act of 1968 with the Fair Housing Amendments Act in 1988. These amendments expanded the rulings of the original act in a number of important ways. No one was permitted to discriminate with housing because of an individual's disability or based on their family status. This meant that home sellers or renters could not disallow families with pregnant women or who had children less than 18 years of age living with them.

To prevent disability discrimination, the act included construction and design accessibility rules for some multifamily homes. Those that were to be occupied initially after March 13, 1991 had to comply with the accessibility provisions for disabled people.

The amendments also created new means of enforcing and administering the rules. HUD Housing and Urban Development attorneys were now able to take cases to administrative law judges for victims of such housing discrimination. The jurisdiction of the Justice Department became expanded and revised in such a way that it could file suits in Federal district courts for discrimination victims.

HUD has been tasked with the principal responsible to administer the Fair Housing Act of 1968 since the government adopted it. Thanks to the amendments in 1988, the department has become substantially more involved in enforcing the provisions. This is because the newly protected families and disabled brought many new complaints. The department also had to move beyond investigating and conciliating. They were tasked with mandatory enforcing the rules.

Any complaint regarding the Fair Housing Act of 1968 that individuals file with HUD becomes investigated. The FHEO Fair Housing and Equal Opportunity office handles this responsibility. When complaints can not be resolved voluntarily, the FHEO decides if there is sufficient evidence for a reasonable case of discrimination in housing practices. If they find reasonable cause, then HUD issues a Determination and Charge of Discrimination to the complaint parties. Hearings are next scheduled in front of a law judge for the HUD administration. Either the complaining party or the accused can terminate this procedure to instead have the matter resolved in Federal courts.

At this point, the Department of Justice assumes HUD's responsibility for the aggrieved party's complaints. They act as counsel that seeks to resolve the charges. The matter then becomes a civil case. In either the case of the HUD law judge hearing or the civil action held in the courts, the U.S. Court of Appeals can review the outcome.

The Fair Housing Act of 1968 proved to be historic as the final major act in the civil rights movement legislation. Despite this, housing remained segregated throughout much of the United States for decades. During the thirty years from 1950 through 1980, America's urban centers' black population grew from 6.1 million up to 15.3 million people.

At the same time, white Americans continuously abandoned the cities in favor of the suburbs. With them went a great number of the jobs that the black population needed to communities where they did not find welcome. The result of this ongoing trend caused urban America to be filled with ghettos. These are the communities inside the American inner cities where many minority populations live. They have been dogged by consistently high crime, unemployment, drug use, and other social problems.

Fed Funds Rate

Fed Funds Rate refers to the most key interest rate benchmark in the United States. Such a benchmark rate is the one which the banks charge one another in order to borrow money from each other overnight. The Federal Reserve similarly deploys this rate as a tool in order to meaningfully impact monetary policy within the country. This is not the only benchmark rate in America today, yet it has no rival for importance.

The way the Federal Reserve is able to influence banks with it is somewhat complicated. The commercial banks must maintain a minimum level of money either in cash funds or with their particular regional branch of the Federal Reserve on deposit. The idea behind this is that it allows banks to meet customer withdrawals from their current accounts, including both checking and savings.

Sensible banks hold more than this bare minimum. They keep an excess of the reserves that the regulations and rules pertaining to the banking universe require. These are appropriately referred to as excess reserves. It is such excess reserves that the Fed Funds Rate directly affects.

As the better prepared banks keep plenty of excess reserves available, they are able to overnight loan out to the less prepared banks so that they can end business day operations at their legally required minimum obligation. This unsecured overnight loan occurs at the Fed Funds Rate. It represents the effective rate that the lending bank will charge the borrowing bank.

In nearly all cases, this Fed Funds Rate proves to be the lowest practical interest rate in the nation. Since the financial crisis, it has remained at slightly higher than zero percent. The Federal Reserve began increasing it with their first rate hike in December of 2015, both slowly and gradually.

This rate matters for more reasons than just the price at which a lending bank will charge a borrowing bank to utilize its excess reserves. The reason is that the Federal Reserve is able to set their monetary policy with the rate. As an example, they might decide they need to cut the effective rate of unemployment in the U.S. This is one of their two reasons for existing (along with keeping inflation low). In order to increase employment opportunities, the Fed will push down the Fed Funds Rate through purchasing securities off of commercial banks. As bank reserves go up, the price for them declines. This is their means for pushing down the federal funds rate.

A lower Fed Funds Rate means that banks try to find better opportunities to engage their excess reserves. They might do this by loaning out the money to individuals who seek to purchase a house. They could also lend the cash to companies interested in expanding their business. Either of these actions will boost the economy in some meaningful way. A more active economy will create more jobs and drive down the unemployment rate.

Besides this, the banks also employ the Fed Funds Rate as their basing benchmark from which they determine their other key interest rates. Once the Federal Reserve boosted their federal funds rate target back in December of 2016 as an example, each of the main banks in the country instantly increased their prime loan lending rates. These represent those rates which they offer to their best customers who are extremely creditworthy. The best customers are usually the large and economically powerful MNC multinational corporations.

This means that the effective Fed Funds Rate is not simply the one that the banks are paying each other when they borrow excess reserves from one another. Instead, it has a dramatic and literal connection to the rate of interest any individual will pay for a car loan, home equity loan or line of credit, and mortgage. It also impacts the price that companies will pay to build and grow their business using bank loans.

Fiat Money

Fiat Money proves to be money that has no real intrinsic, or actual, value. It instead derives its worth from governments accepting it as legal tender. The concept of fiat money on a large scale is a relatively new one. Throughout practically all of history, the majority of currencies around the world derived their value from silver or gold. Fiat money is instead entirely based on trust and faith in the issuing monetary authority.

The problem with fiat money lies in the ability of the governments to inflate its value away. They can do this by over printing it. Since fiat currencies are not restricted by a requirement of hard reserve assets, they can be created in any quantity that the issuing government desires. As the supply continues to rise while the demand remains constant, its purchasing power will fall. When the supply is drastically increased, then hyperinflation will result. Fiat money that falls by hundreds of percent in value is deemed to be a victim of hyperinflation.

The other disadvantage is that only peoples' trust in it ultimately gives it practical value. It suffers from inflation and finally hyperinflation, then the confidence in it becomes shaken. Fiat money that lacks the confidence of its citizens will finally collapse in value and then no longer be of any trading use for daily transactions. When it fails, people either return to barter systems, or the government establishes a currency based on hard assets once again.

The history of money has proven on a number of occasions that governments debase currency to the point of fiat money when it suits them. They do this because it allows them to print as much as they need to pay for things. While this creates inflation for their citizens, it gives the money issuing government the ability to repay their debts with cheaper fiat money. Finally, as a society has had enough of the devalued money and currency instability, they force the government to return to asset backed money. This has happened before, and some monetary experts say that you are starting to see this happen again nowadays.

FICO Score

FICO Score refers to the overwhelmingly most popular and heavily utilized credit score in the United States. The company which created, owns, and manages it to this day is Fair Isaac Corporation. Financial institutions that loan out money employ this FICO score for an individual to assess any credit risk and decide whether or not they will offer the person credit. Sometimes they also consider specific information on the credit report of the borrower, but this is increasingly uncommon.

The reason for this is that the FICO score contemplates a well-rounded set of risk parameters for the would-be borrowers. These five areas it considers and draws upon to issue a credit score for credit worthiness include the individual's payment history, present amount of debts, types of credit utilized, amount of credit history, and new credit inquiries and issued accounts.

Ninety percent of financial institutions in the United States that offer loans rely on the FICO score for assessing the creditworthiness of an individual. These scores vary from as low as 300 to as high as 850. Generally speaking, scores over 650 represent desirable credit history. Individuals who boast less than 620 conversely typically find it hard to get decent financing offers approved at reasonable interest rates. Financial institutions claim that they also consider various other details besides FICO scores. These include history of time at a job, applicant's income, and the kind of credit they are seeking.

It is interesting and illuminating to understand how the three main credit bureaus calculate this FICO Score. Fair Isaac Corporation has its proprietary model in which they weigh all categories differently for every individual. This makes it more difficult to say with certainty what percentages in each of the five categories they consider.

Yet generally speaking, payment history represents 35 percent of the total. Amount owed on accounts comprises 30 percent generally. Amount of years of credit history equals approximately 15 percent. Credit mix equates to around 10 percent. New credit inquiries and accounts represent about 10 percent.

Payment history is the simple answer to the question, "does the individual borrower pay the accounts in a timely fashion?" Thanks to the exhaustive nature of credit history, the bureaus clearly demonstrate the payments which have been made for every single line of credit. The reports make special note if any of the payments came in 30, 60, 90, 120, or still more days later than due.

Amounts owed on accounts pertains to the dollar amounts individuals owe on their various accounts as a percentage of the total available credit. This does not mean that possessing a great amount of debt ruins a credit score. What the Fair Isaac Company is considering is the ratio of amount owed to amount available. A clear example shows that when Ringo owed $100,000 yet was not near his limits on any of the accounts, he had a higher credit score than George who only owed $25,000 yet had nearly maxed out his credit card accounts.

Credit history length is a complex category. FICO considers the age of the oldest account as well as the age of the most recent one. They then compile the average account age and come up with a value for this category. Those with shorter credit histories can still get a good credit score.

Credit mix pertains to the variety in types of credit accounts. Higher category credit scores go to those people who have a strong and varied mix of credit cards, retail accounts, and installment loans like mortgages, vehicle loans, and signature loans.

Finally, the Fair Isaac Company does not like recently opened accounts in much of any quantity. When borrowers take out a range of new credit lines and accounts in only a brief amount of time, this tells them that the person is becoming a credit risk and thus decreases the total FICO score.

Financial Mentor

A financial mentor is a trusted guide or counselor that helps a person in the arena of business, personal finance and investments. Mentors can be many different people, but they typically have several characteristics in common. They are all loyal advisers who have the person's best interests at heart.

Mentoring is most widely used in business. Other settings that use it include medical fields and educational settings. Business experts will tell you that among the most useful, helpful, and valuable career assets that you can have in your business career is a helpful and experienced mentor.

Financial mentors are commonly older individuals who have more wisdom and experience to share with the individual than he or she already possesses. Though they do not have to be older in every single case, they must always have more experience than the person whom they are mentoring. These mentors both guide financial development and assist the person with their overall financial and business goals. They do not engage in this process with the expressed intent of making money or benefiting financially from the arrangement usually.

With financial mentors, you as the person being mentored have some preparation that you can do. You should listen carefully to the mentor and what he or she has to tell you. This is most easily accomplished by coming to the meeting with the financial mentor with some sort of recording means prepared. This might be a voice recorder, PDA, laptop, or even pen and paper. If a mentor made specific recommendations in the prior discussions, then you should have both noted and tried to apply them. Be ready to review any steps that you have taken specifically with the mentor.

You should also allow a mentor to be a part of your big picture goals and plans, and not only the particular details. The overall goals for you who are being mentored should be set together, in conjunction with the mentor. They should talk not only about present challenges and difficulties, but also concentrate on long term and short term goals together.

Good financial mentors will also do more than simply hold official meetings. They will take the time to get to know you. This does not have to be extensive amounts of time, but it should be quality time spent. This might involve a fifteen minute friendly chat over coffee or a quick bite to eat out some night. The key is not to take up too much of the financial mentor's time until you get to know him or her better. Then as the relationship broadens out into a friendship, more opportunities to get together will naturally arise.

Financial mentors can help out with many areas of your life. They can make helpful suggestions for getting out of debt. They can guide you with good concepts for practical and smart investing. They can share personal, actual experience for navigating through difficulties with a business that you own. They might suggest advice to assist you in your career development. Whatever help that you specifically request from a mentor, you should always remember to be appreciative and take the time to write thank you notes.

Financial Statement

Financial statements are official records of a business' or personal financial activity. With businesses, financial statements present any and all pertinent financial activity as usable information. They do this in a clear, organized, and simple to comprehend way.

Financial statements are commonly comprised of four different types of financial accounts that come with an analysis and discussion provided by the company's management. The Balance sheet is the first of these. It is known by several other names, including statement of financial condition, or statement of financial position. The balance sheet details will outline a corporation's ownership equity, liabilities, and assets on a particular date. This will give a good picture of the general strength and position of the company.

Financial statements similarly include income statements. These can also be called Profit and Loss statements too. They outline numerous important pieces of company information, such as corporate expenses, income, and profits made in a certain time period. This statement explains all of the relevant financial details to the business' operation. Sales and all associated expenses are included under this category. This section of the financial statement proves to be the nuts and bolts of the whole document. It provides a snap shot of the company's ability to generate sales and turn profits.

A statement of cash flow is also a part of a complete financial statement. As its name implies, this section will share all of the details regarding the company's activities pertaining to cash flow. The most important ones that will be outlined include operating cash flow, financing, and investing endeavors.

The last element of a financial statement includes the statement of retained earnings. This section of the document makes good on its name to detail any changes to a corporation's actual retained earnings for the period that is being reported. These four sections of a financial statement are all combined together to make the consolidated financial statement, once they are combined with the analysis and discussion of management.

With large multinational types of corporations, such financial statements are typically large and complicated, making them challenging to read and understand. To assist with readability, they may also come with a group of notes for the financial statement that also covers management's analysis and discussion. Such notes will go through all items listed on the four parts of the financial statement in more thorough detail. For many companies, these notes for financial statements have come to be deemed a critical component of good and complete financial statements.

Financial statements are used by several different groups of people who are looking at a company. Investors use them in order to determine if the company and its stocks or bonds make a sound investment with a chance of providing good returns on investments and profits in exchange for limited risks. Banks utilize these financial statements to decide if a company is a good credit risk for their loan dollars. Institutions and other groups that may be considering a cash infusion or buyout of the company use such financial statements to decide if the company is a viable investment or acquisition target.

Gold Roth IRA

Gold Roth IRA's are IRA's that are allowed to contain gold and other precious metals. Gold Roth IRA's make sense for many investors. This is because gold and other precious metals like silver and platinum have been considered to be the greatest form of long term storage for cash and valuables throughout history.

This means that gold in particular could be considered to be the best asset for retirement. Although there are many other types of instruments used for retirement accounts and planning, including bonds, stocks, savings, and annuities, gold is the only one whose final value does not rest on an institution or individual's performance or success. This makes physical gold an ideal means for saving for retirement.

Gold Roth IRA's are specially created either through initially funding one or by rolling over a Roth IRA or traditional IRA to a gold backed Roth IRA. Rolling over an existing employee held 401K to a Gold Roth IRA can be difficult if the employee has not left the company. This is because employees are not usually allowed to do rollovers until they separate from their company.

IRA's that already exist can be transferred to Gold Roth IRA's. They can be moved from credit unions, banks, or stock broker firms to a trust company that is allowed to hold your Gold IRA holdings. In this type of transfer, you could choose to move securities held in the account along with cash, or cash by itself.

Gold Roth IRA's must be created by sending in cash to the administrator of the IRA. They will then purchase the gold, silver, or platinum physical holdings as you instruct them. The gold must then be kept by a gold IRA custodian on your behalf. These depositories provide safe places for the gold, as well as easy access to buy or sell it. The gold kept in a Gold Roth IRA may not be sent to your house or assumed in your personal possession. Instead, it has to be liquidated before the funds from it can be accessed. Gold that is requested as a distribution will be penalized at your personal tax rate plus a ten percent penalty.

Only certain forms of gold and precious metals are allowed to be purchased and held within a Gold Roth IRA. Gold bars have to demonstrate a twenty-four karat purity to be eligible. They can be one ounce, ten ounces, a kilogram, one hundred ounces, or four hundred ounces in size. Gold coins that are permitted are twenty-four karat bullion coins from the United States, Canada, Austria, and Australia. The most heavily minted gold coins of all time, the South Africa Krugerrand's, are not permitted, as they are only twenty-two karats.

Silver bars and coins that have .999 or higher purity are permitted to be held in a Gold Roth IRA account. This allows the Canadian Silver Maple Leaf, the U.S. Silver Eagle, and the Mexican Silver Libertad one ounce bullion coins. Silver bars that are one hundred ounces and one thousand ounces are also permitted.

Good Debt

Good debt is debt that benefits a person or business to carry. Such good debts demonstrate both the creditworthiness and the responsibility of a borrower. They also create a good base to build on in the future. There are many examples of good debt, which stands in contrast to bad debt.

Good debts are typically those debts that are taken on to acquire an item or investment that only grows in value with time. Examples of this include things like real estate loans, schooling loans, home mortgages, business debt, and passive income investments. Each of these items could provide a significant and real advantage with time. Real estate could increase in value and be resold for profits.

Higher education commonly leads to greater amounts of earnings. Loans on homes are commonly wonderful for building credit and provide properties that serve as excellent collateral. Loans for businesses may result in profits earned from trade and sales. It is important to note that cars and other items are not included in these lists. This is simply because they lose value the moment that they are purchased and driven away.

Bad debts in contrast are those that result in higher interest rates and considerable deprecation of the items purchased with time. Goods that are for short time frame use and bought on credit are commonly considered to be bad debts. Since the item's life span will only decline with time, and the interest rates are typically high, no benefit is derived from purchasing these things with debt. A great number of such purchases rapidly decline in value, even after one use.

A significant benefit to good debts lies in the increase in cash flow that they commonly create. Properly structured good debts lead to tax advantages, to the ability to invest in still more assets that can produce cash, and to higher credit scores as well. Good debts that are paid on time furthermore build up a good financial base for the future. Good debts create cash flow, which stands in contrast to bad debts that do not.

Investments that produce passive income are among the best good debts. For example, purchasing an apartment building using debt will result in both income revenue and substantial tax deductions. This proves to be good debt, since although you are borrowing money, you are receiving passive income and gaining the ability to depreciate assets that can actually appreciate with time. On top of this, you are allowed to live there while you accrue all of these other benefits.

When considering a good debt, you should make certain that the income that the investment will provide is high enough to make the investment and the accompanying debt worth while. A number of experts offer advice on this. They suggest that not tying up in excess of twenty percent of your overall value in debt is a better practice. Higher debt levels than this can sound off warning bells with banks and other lenders.

Home Equity

Home Equity refers to those assets which result from the home owner's stake in the house itself. Calculating up the equity of the home is not difficult. One simply takes any remaining loan balances and subtracts them off of the market value of the property. It is very possible for the equity in a home to grow with time, in particular when the value of the property rises and also as the balance of the loan becomes gradually paid down over time.

An easier way to think of this home equity is as the part of the property which the home owner actually owns. The lender is always the interest holder in a given property that includes a mortgage secured by the home. This is the case all the way up to the point where the home owner pays off completely the mortgage loan balance. It is no exaggeration to state that the equity in a home is commonly the most valuable asset for most home buyers. Equity in a home allows for a home owner to take out a second mortgage at later points in the life of the mortgage loan.

It is always helpful to look at a real-world example to better understand difficult and challenging concepts such as this one. If a home buyer obtained a house for $250,000 and dutifully made a full 20 percent down payment, then he would likely obtain a $200,000 mortgage loan to pay the remaining balance on the house. The home equity at this initial point would equate to the down payment of $50,000. The home's value is $250,000, but the buyer only contributed $50,000 as an upfront down payment towards the purchase price.

In the unlikely event that the value of the home doubled, it would then be worth $500,000. Yet despite this windfall increase in value, the mortgage is still only $200,000. This would mean that the home equity increased to a massive $300,000. The equity stake then would have risen to 60 percent. Figuring this up is simply a function of dividing the balance of the loan by the market value to subtract the end result from one. Then the person must convert the resulting decimal into a percentage. While the balance on the mortgage has not grown, the equity in the home has massively increased.

There are several ways that a home owner might increase the equity within his home. The simplest way is to pay down the loan balance at a faster rate than only the monthly mortgage payment amounts. Slowly over time, these monthly payments will go more and more towards the principal repayment. It means that all else being equal, a person builds up the equity in the home at a rate that increases gradually every year. By making extra payments each month, which all accrue against the principal only, this equity grows faster and eventually exponentially so.

Another way equity accrues to a home is through home price appreciation. As the home grows in value (thanks to natural area appreciation or home improvement projects) the equity in the property similarly grows. Equity is always a handy asset, which makes it an integral part of the person's aggregate net worth. In an emergency or on a rainy day, home owners can simply withdraw large lump sum amounts from the equity of the house one day. This wealth might also be simply passed along down the family line to the owners' heirs as well.

There are two principle ways to withdraw the equity value from a house. It might be taken as a home equity loan or a home equity line of credit (called a HELOC). Either one will allow an individual to utilize the proceeds for practically anything they wish. This might be for home improvements, vacations, retirement, or university level education as a few examples.

Home Equity Line of Credit (HELOC)

A home equity line of credit is also known by its acronym HELOC. It represents a viable alternative to the more commonly used home equity loan. Whereas home equity loans provide lump sum amounts, Home Equity Lines of Credit provide cash as and when the borrower needs it. The downside to a HELOC is that a bank can decide to reduce the amount of available credit or cancel the line altogether without warning. This can happen before a borrower has utilized the funds.

In a home equity line of credit, borrowers use the equity within the home to be their collateral with the bank. The lending institution decides on the maximum amount that the borrower can obtain. The home owner then determines how much of this they want to borrow for the amount of time the bank permits. This might be until the monthly payments reduce the line to a zero balance, or it could be for a certain number of months. This makes these HELOCs much like a credit card in the ability to draw on the resources only when and as they need them.

The main difference between a home equity line of credit and a home loan is that the former is a revolving loan instrument. Borrowers are able to use the money then pay it off. They can then draw on it once again. Home equity loans pay a single lump sum up front amount one time. HELOCs also feature variable interest rates that will change over time, while home equity loans come with interest rates that are fixed. The payment amounts on the home equity loans are also fixed every month, while the payment on the HELOC depends on how much of the line is used.

In order to be able to obtain a home equity line of credit, the home owner must have significant equity in the house itself. Banks will insist that owners keep at least 10% to 20% equity within the property all the time. This must be the case after the line is approved as well. The HELOC approval process will also require verifiable proof of income, consistent documented employment, and a high credit score that is generally more than 680.

It is important for prospective borrowers to determine what they will use the home equity line of credit money for before they draw on it. Home renovations lend themselves better to home equity loans. This is because the one time large amount would enable the borrower to finish the renovations and then repay the loan. A HELOC is a better fit for a revolving bill such as the children's college tuition. Borrowers can use them to cover the tuition, then pay them off hopefully before the next tuition payment become due. At this point they can re-utilize the HELOC for the next semester tuition.

The home equity line of credit can also be a good choice for individuals who wish to consolidate the balances on their credit cards which feature high interest rates. The rates for the HELOC are typically much lower. This strategy requires some discipline. Once the credit cards have been cleared, there is the danger that the home owner might be tempted to run them back up again while they are still making payments on the line of credit. This would put borrowers in a worse situation than before they chose to consolidate.

Home equity lines of credit can get a home owner into the bad habit of constantly borrowing and paying them back as with a credit card. This can be a problem if the borrowers take on more debt with the HELOC than they can afford to pay in monthly payments. Missing these payments would put their home at jeopardy of being seized by the bank.

Home Equity Loan

A home equity loan is a means for home owners to borrow money using the value of their house. Borrowers find these loans appealing because they can usually borrow significant sums of money. Besides this, they are much simpler to get approved for than with many competing kinds of loans. A home owner's house secures these home equity loans. The borrowers may utilize these funds for any purpose that they wish. They do not have to be spent on expenses related to the house that secures the loan.

Such a home equity loan is actually a kind of second mortgage on a house. The first mortgage allows the buyer to purchase the home. When sufficient equity is established in the house, owners can attach other loans to the property to borrow against it.

There are a number of benefits to obtaining a home equity loan. They appeal to both lenders and borrowers. Borrowers get better APRs or interest rates from them than with other loan types. Because they are secured by the value of the home, they can be easier to get approved for even with bad credit. The IRS allows home owners to deduct interest expenses from these home equity loans from their taxes. Finally, borrowers are able to obtain substantial loan amounts using these loan vehicles.

The lenders like these loans because they consider them to be safer loans. The house acts as collateral in the process. This means that banks are able to seize the house to liquidate it and regain unpaid balances if the owner fails to make the payments. Because of this, banks know that borrowers will make the payments of these loans a high priority so they do not lose their house.

Banks protect themselves in any case by not lending too much against the value of the property. In general, lenders will not allow borrowers to obtain a greater amount than 85% of the value of the house. This includes both the amount that remains on the first mortgage as well as the second mortgage home equity loan. This percentage is known as the loan to value ratio. It can vary somewhat from one bank to the next.

The way home equity loans work is relatively straightforward. Borrowers receive a one time cash payment. They then make fixed payments each month to pay back the loan over a pre-set amount of time. The interest rate will be set by the bank at the beginning of the loan. With every payment, the loan balance declines after part of the interest costs are covered. This makes these amortizing loans.

Sometimes borrowers do not require all of the money at one time. An alternative to the home equity loan in this case is the HELOC home equity line of credit. This delivers a set amount of money which home owners can draw on only when and if they require it. The borrowers only have to pay interest on money which they physically draw and borrow. It is possible for the interest rate to change on these HELOC loans. Banks may also cancel such a line of credit before the borrower has utilized all or part of the funds.

Home equity loans can be used for many different needs. It is wise to improve the value of the house with the money through renovating, remodeling, or increasing the appeal of the property. Other common uses borrowers employ them for are to help pay for a second home, to afford college tuition and expenses for family members, or to consolidate bills with high interest rates.

Hyperinflation

In the field of economics, hyperinflation proves to be inflation, or rising prices over time, that is extremely high and even beyond controlling. This state of the economy exists as the overall levels of pricing in a certain country are rising sharply and quickly at the same time as the actual values of these economic goods remain roughly the same price as measured in other more stable currencies. In other words, the nation's own currency is diminishing in value rapidly, commonly at rate that grows in pace.

The IASB, or International Accounting Standards Board, gives a precise definition of hyperinflation. They state that when the rate of inflation during three cumulative years nears one hundred percent total, or at least twenty-six percent each year compounded annually for three consecutive years, then hyperinflation has been reached. Other economists such as Cagan have declared hyperinflation to be when inflation is greater than fifty percent each month. Hyperinflation can witness the overall price levels go up by five to ten percent and higher even in single days for extended periods of time. This stands in sharp contrast to regular inflation which is commonly only reported over a quarterly or annual basis.

As greater and greater amounts of inflation are created in each printing of money instance, a truly vicious cycle takes effect. Such hyperinflation is clearly evident as the money supply grows at an uninterrupted rate. It is typically seen alongside the population's unwillingness to keep the hyper-inflationary currency for any longer than they have to in order to use it for any hard good that will prevent them from losing more actual purchasing power. Hyperinflation is typically a part of wars and their after effects, social or political upheavals, and currency meltdowns such as seen in Zimbabwe.

Hyperinflation is a phenomenon that is unique to fiat currencies that are not backed up by anything but a government's faith and trust. As the money supply is not limited by normal restraints like gold in a vault, it is instead run by a paper money standard. The supply of it is completely dependent on the discretion of the government.

Hyperinflation commonly leads to intense and long lasting economic depressions. This is not always the case though. In Brazil which suffered in the grips of hyperinflation for thirty years in the 1964 to 1994 period, the government managed to avoid economic collapse by valuing all non-monetary goods, services, and investments for the whole economy in an involved index. The government supplied this daily updated index that they measured with the daily Brazilian currency against the United States dollar.

In contrast to Brazil, Zimbabwe did not bother to set up such an index measured against the dollar. They did offer the day by day changes in the U.S. dollar as a comparison for everyone in the country to see. This voluntary comparison only served to worsen the problem and finally destroyed the real value of non monetary items that did not get updated as expressed against the Zimbabwe dollar. All monetary items in the country finally lost every bit of value during the hyper-inflationary meltdown.

Income Statement

An Income Statement refers to a corporate financial statement that relays the performance of the company for a specific accounting time frame. Analysts measure such performance through reading the summary of the business revenues and expenditures in its non-operating and operating endeavors together. This statement reveals the net loss or net profit which the business experienced in the particular accounting time period. These documents are also referred to as statements of revenues or profit and loss statements.

As one of three important financial statements, these become contained within the yearly 10-K and corporate annual reports. The other two critical documents are the statement of cash flows and the balance sheet. Every publically traded firm is required by law to deliver such legal documents to the investing public via the SEC Securities and Exchange Commission. These three combined statements relay all of the critical information on the firm's financial affairs. Yet the income statement is special in that it alone reveals the company's net income and overall sales' overviews.

Income statements are different from the balance sheet in at least one critical way. Balance sheets provide a single moment in time snap shot of corporate performance. Income statements on the other hand deliver useful information on an entire time frame or period. They start with the company sales figures and conclude with the total net income and appropriate EPS earnings per share figures.

These income statements become sub-divided into two sections. The first is operating. The second proves to be non-operating. Operating sections of the statements on income reveal all of the pertinent data on expenses and revenues which result directly from the normal principal daily operations of the business. It helps to look at a real world example to better understand the concept. If a company makes computer equipment, then it will mostly earn its revenues through manufacturing and selling such computer equipment.

In the non-operating segment of the income statement, investors learn about the expenses and revenues associated with extraordinary operations of the firm. Continuing on with the prior example, the computer equipment firm may also sell some investments and real estate properties. Any and all gains it realizes on the sales would be included under the non-operating items portion of the statement.

Analysts find a number of important uses for these income statements. Among the key ones is figuring up critical financial ratios like ROA return on assets, ROE return on equity, gross and operating profits, EVIT earnings before interest and taxes, and EBITDA earnings before interest, taxes, and amortization. As such, these statements will commonly be portrayed in a standardized format that lays out every line item as a percentage of the sales. This method allows for analysts and investors alike to quickly and easily determine the expenses that comprise the greatest amount of the sales.

These statements may similarly compare and contrast both the QOQ quarter over quarter performance and the YOY year over year performance. This is why the income statement commonly delivers at least two and often three years of comparable historical data for analysts to consider. There are also two methods for presenting the income statements. They might be offered in a multi-step format. Accountants for the company could also portray them in a single step format. Each of the two methods is consistent with the important GAAP standards. They also both provide the identical net income final numbers. In fact their figures are formulated in more or less the same way. It is only their compilation and format which proves to be different from one another.

Income Tax

Income tax refers to the tax on income which governments mandate for all personal and business entities and organizations which reside or are based in their jurisdiction. The law states that both individuals and businesses have to file their income tax returns once each year. Such filing demonstrates if they owe the government taxes or are instead able to claim a tax refund. This makes the tax on income a critical source of funding for governments. They employ it to pay for their various activities, goods, and services which they provide to the citizens and residents of their home country.

Income tax systems are usually progressive in nature. This is because national governments tend to understand that higher income earners have the broadest shoulders to bear the heaviest burdens of higher tax rates. The lower income earning individuals (and businesses) can not pay so much of their gross incomes.

The United States first imposed an income tax on its citizens in the time of the War of 1812. The goal for this tax was only to help repay the still-fledgling nation's $100 million worth of debt. They ran this up in the expenses related to the costly war on both land and sea. The government actually made good on its promise to repeal this tax on income after the conclusion of the war and repayment of the national war debt.

Despite this fact, income tax in America became a permanent fixture in the country in the early years of the twentieth century. The United States' entry into the First World War especially ran up enormous costs and debts for the nation. The tax never again disappeared in the U.S. The story is similar in many Western economically developed nations such as Great Britain, Canada, and others.

Within the U.S. today, it is the IRS Internal Revenue Service which carries the responsibility of enforcing tax laws and collecting these income taxes. They utilize a complicated and bureaucratic system of regulations and rules on incomes that have to be reported. They also monitor and decide which credits and deductions those filing individuals and businesses may claim. This agency collects the taxes from any type of income including wages, commissions, salaries, bonuses, investment earnings, and business income.

Individual income tax is one of the largest revenue generators for the Federal government of the United States today. The majority of citizens and residents within the country do not have to pay taxes on the entirety of their full earnings. Instead, the government utilizes a system of deductions on many different items to reduce the people's taxable income. Among these important deductions are dental and medical bills, interest on a mortgage, and educational expenses.

Taxpayers are allowed to minus these from their gross income in order to decide how much of their income is actually taxable. Should a taxpayer make $120,000 income and receive $20,000 worth of deductions, then the IRS will only impose taxes on the remainder of $100,000. After this, the tax agency will apply credits against the taxes which individuals owe. This means that an individual who owed $25,000 worth of taxes and received $5,000 in credits will only have to pay $20,000 total taxes.

Besides federal income taxes, a great number of the fifty states within the U.S. also collect their own state income taxes. Only seven states did not levy such taxes on their residents as of 2016. These lucky state residents lived in Wyoming, Washington state, Texas, South Dakota, Nevada, Florida, and Alaska. The two states of Tennessee and New Hampshire only levy such income taxes on any earnings realized from investments and dividends.

Businesses and corporations must also pay taxes on their earnings. The IRS deems any type of partnerships, corporations, small businesses, and even self-employed contractors to be businesses. Such groups must first report all of their business income and then subtract out their capital and operating expenses. What remains is called taxable business income.

Inflation

Inflation proves to be prices rising over time. It is specifically measured as the increase in a given basket of goods and services' prices. These goods and services are taken to represent the entire economy. Inflation is also the going up in cost of the average prices of goods and services as measured by the CPI, or consumer price index. The opposite of inflation is known as deflation. Deflation turns out to be the falling of an average level of prices. The point that separates the two from each other, both deflation and inflation, is price stability, or no change in the costs of goods and services.

Inflation has almost everything to do with the amount of money available. It is inextricably tied to the money supply. This gives rise to the popularly remarked observation that inflation is actually an excessive number of dollars chasing too small a quantity of goods. Comprehending the way that this works is easier when considering an example.

Pretend for a moment that the world possessed only two commodities: oranges that are gathered up from orange trees and paper money created by government. In seasons where rain is limited and the oranges are few as a result, the cost of oranges should go up. This is because the same number of printed dollars would be competing for a smaller number of oranges.

On the other hand, if a bumper crop of oranges are seen, then the cost of oranges should drop, since the sellers of oranges have no choice but to cut prices to sell off their large inventory of oranges. These two examples illustrate inflation in the former and deflation in the latter. The main difference between the real world and this example is that inflation measures changes in the price movement on average of many or all goods and services, and not simply one.

The quantity of money in an economy similarly impacts the amount of inflation present at any given time. Should the government in the example above choose to print enormous amounts of money, then there will be many dollars for a relatively constant number of oranges, as in the lack of rain scenario. So inflation is created by the number of dollars going up against the quantities of oranges that exist, or overall goods and services existing. Deflation, as the opposite of inflation, would be the numbers of dollars dropping compared to the quantity of oranges available.

Because of this, levels of inflation result from four different factors that often work together in combination. The demand for money could drop. The supply of money could expand. The available supply of various other goods might decline. Finally, the demand for other goods increases.

Even though these four factors do work in correlation, economists say that inflation is mostly a currency driven event. This means that in the vast majority of cases, it results from governments tampering with the money supply. Generally, they do this by over printing their own currency to have money to pay for spending, resulting in higher inflation.

Initial Public Offering (IPO)

An IPO is the acronym for an Initial Public Offering. Such IPO's represent the first opportunity for most investors to start buying shares of stock in the firm in question. Initial Public Offerings commonly generate a great deal of excitement, not only for the company involved but also for the members of the investing community.

Private companies decide to issue stock and become publicly traded companies for a few different reasons. The main two motivating factors revolve around the need to raise more capital, as well as the desire to permit the original business owners and investors to take profits on their time and investment that they originally put into starting up the company.

It is true that private companies are limited in the amount of capital that they are able to raise, since their ownership turns out to be restricted to certain organizations and individuals. Public companies have the advantages of allowing any investor to take a stake through buying stock shares on exchanges that are publicly traded. It is far easier for them to raise money as public companies.

Initial Public Offerings that go well translate to large amounts of cash for a company. They use this for future expansion and development. Those who began the company or who were initial investors typically make enormous gains at that time in compensation for their time and effort.

Initial Public Offerings take huge amounts of preliminary work. Great amounts of paper work have to be filled in and filed with the regulatory oversight groups. A prospectus has to be created for investors to study and consider. Advertising campaigns for the first shares that will be sold must be developed. On top of these tasks, the company has to continue its normal operations. Because of this, financial firms such as Morgan Stanley or Goldman Sachs are commonly engaged to perform these tasks on the company's behalf. Such a firm is called the IPO underwriting company. With enormous sized IPO's, these tasks could even be divided up between a few different IPO underwriting companies.

Contrary to what many people think, the majority of IPO's typically do not do well initially. Besides this, a percentage of the companies will not make it, meaning that all of the investment in the IPO stock could be lost. Because of this, there is great risk and often lower rewards for sinking money into Initial Public Offerings than in traditional well established companies and stocks. Many investors buy into the enthusiasm and excitement that surrounds Initial Public Offerings. Another explanation for their euphoria may have to do with believing that there is something special in being among the first investors to acquire the next possible Apple, Coca Cola, or IBM. Whatever their reasoning proves to be, investors continue to love Initial Public Offerings and the somewhat long shot opportunities that they represent.

Interest Rate

Interest rates are the levels at which interest is charged a borrower for using money that they obtain in the form of a loan from a bank or other lender. These are also the rates that individuals and businesses are paid for depositing their funds with a bank. Interest rates are central to the running of capitalist economies. They are commonly written out as percentage rates for a given time frame, most commonly per year.

As an example, a small business might require capital to purchase new assets for the company. To acquire these, they borrow money form a bank. In exchange for making them this loan, the bank is paid interest at a pre set and agreed upon rate of interest for lending it to the company and putting off their own use of the monies. They receive this interest in monthly payments along with repayments of the principal.

Interest rates are also used by government agencies in pursuing monetary policies. Central banks set them to influence their nation's economic performance. They impact many elements of an economy such as unemployment, inflation, and investment levels.

There are several different interest rates to consider. The most commonly expressed one is the nominal interest rate. This nominal interest rate proves to be the amount of interest that is payable in money terms. If a family deposits $1,000 in a bank for a year, and is paid $50 in interest, then their balance by the conclusion of the year will be $1,050. This would translate to a nominal interest rate amounting to five percent per year.

The real interest rate is another type of rate used to determine how much purchasing power is received. It is the interest rate after the level of inflation is subtracted. Determining the real interest rate is a matter of calculating the nominal rate and removing the amount of inflation from it. In the example above, supposed the economy's inflation level is measured at five percent for the year. This would mean that the $1,050 in the account at year end only buys what it did as $1,000 at the beginning of the year. This translates to a real interest rate of zero.

Interest rates change for many reasons. They are altered for political gains of parties in power. By reducing the interest rate, an economy gains a short term boost. The help to the economy will often influence the outcome of elections. Unfortunately, the short term advantage gained is often offset later by inflation. This reason for changing interest rates is eliminated with independent central banks.

Another main reason that interest rates change is because of expectations of inflation. Since the majority of economies demonstrate inflation, fixed amounts of money will purchase fewer goods a year from now than they will today. Lenders expect to be compensated for this. Central banks raise interest rates to fight this inflation as necessary.

Intrinsic Value

Intrinsic value has several meanings where finance and business are concerned. The first of these meanings pertains to companies and their underlying stock issues. An intrinsic value of a stock could be said to be the actual per share value of a stock, in contrast to its book value or price according to the stock market.

Intrinsic value takes many other elements into account, such as trademarks and copyrights owned, as well as the value of the brand name. These factors are intangible in nature. This makes it hard to figure out their true worth, although it can be done. As a result of this, such items of intrinsic value are not commonly included in the stock's actual market price.

A different way of understanding intrinsic value is that the intrinsic value is the amount that a company is actually worth. Market capitalization on the other hand is the price that investors will willingly pay for a company at any given point. Intrinsic value can be calculated in varying ways, depending on the investor who is doing the calculation.

Intrinsic value is also the amount of money that a call or put option on a stock is in the money. Call options give investors the right but not the obligation to buy a stock at a certain price, while put options grant investors the right but not obligation to sell a stock at a particular price. Figuring up a call option's intrinsic value is done by simply taking the difference of the call option's strike price and subtracted from the actual price of the underlying stock.

As an example, a call option might have a strike price of $40. The stock that this option is based on could be worth $55 per share. This would give the option an intrinsic value of $15 each share, or $1,500 since stock options represent a hundred shares. Stock prices that prove to be lower than call options do not possess any intrinsic value.

Put option intrinsic values are found by taking the difference of the strike price of the put option and subtracting the price of the stock that underlies them. As an example, should a put option contain a strike price of $30, and the stock be trading at only $25, then the put option will have an intrinsic value of $5 per share, or $500 for the one hundred share option. On the other hand, if the stock market price turned out to be higher than the strike price of this put option, then the option would not contain any intrinsic value.

Intrinsic value is also the true, real worth of an asset or object. Gold and silver have intrinsic value in that people will pay you for them at any time and in any country. Conversely, paper currencies may only be said to have intrinsic value if they are linked to or backed up by a hard asset.

Lease

Leases are contracts made between an owner, or lessor, and a user, or lesee, covering the utilization of an asset. Leases can pertain to business or real estate. There are a variety of different types of leases that vary with the property in question being leased.

Tangible property and assets are leased under rental agreements. Intangible property leases are much like a license, only they have differing provisions. The utilization of a computer program or a cell phone service's radio frequency are two example of such an intangible lease.

A gross lease is another type of lease. In a gross lease, a tenant actually gives a certain defined dollar amount in rent. The landlord is then responsible for any and all property expenses that are routinely necessary in owning the asset. This includes everything from washing machines to lawnmowers.

You also encounter leases that are cancelable. Cancelable leases can be ended at the discretion of the end user or lessor. Other leases are non cancelable and may not be ended ahead of schedule. In daily conversation, a lease denotes a lease that can not be broken, while a rental agreement often can be canceled.

A lease contract typically lays out particular provisions concerning both rights and obligations of the lessor and the lessee. Otherwise, a local law code's provisions will apply. When the holder of the lease, also known as the tenant, pays the arranged fee to the owner of the property, the tenant gains exclusive use and possession of the property that is leased to the point that the owner and any other individuals may not utilize it without the tenant's specific invitation. By far the most typical type of hard property lease proves to be the residential types of rental agreements made between landlords and their tenants. This type of relationship that the two parties establish is also known as a tenancy. The tenant's right to possess the property is many times referred to as the leasehold interest. These leases may exist for pre arranged amounts of time, known as a lease term. In many cases though, they can be terminated in advance, although this does depend on the particular lease's terms and conditions.

Licenses are similar to leases, but not the same thing. The main difference between the two lies in the nature of the ongoing payments and termination. When keeping the property is only accomplished by making regular payments, and can not be terminated unless the money is not paid or some form of misconduct is discovered, then the agreement is a lease. One time uses of or entrances to property are licenses. The defining difference between the two proves to be that leases require routine payments in their term and come with a particular date of ending.

Legal Tender

Legal tender proves to be official forms of payment that the nation's government recognizes for paying either private or public debts or for meeting any number of financial obligations. In nearly all nations, national currency is the one and only legal tender. Creditors have no choice but to receive this currency for repaying of debts owed to them. It is only the appropriately endowed national institutions which are permitted to issue such legal tender. In the United States, this means the U.S. Treasury. In Canada, it refers to the Royal Canadian Mint.

Any type of payment which must be taken for a debt is legal tender. The laws of the land determine which payments are such currencies. This term mostly pertains to money in cash form like coins and bills. It does not include credit cards, bank cards, checks, or lines of credit. Laws which pertain to legal tender are the bedrock in the forming of a country's fiscal policy for a great number of states.

In the days of the American federalist debates, individuals who sought to restrict the powers of the new central government attempted to force rules restricting the creation of a national central bank and to ensure that the national government could not issue currency. Such positions as those espoused by the anti-federalists were mostly defeated. The U.S. Constitution does in fact forbid individual states from issuing their own currencies, meaning they obtained at least a partial state-level victory.

Following the American war for independence, the fledgling nation utilized a wide range of foreign silver and gold coins in trade. Throughout the American Civil War, these policies had to be altered because of the enormous levels of government debt issued and assumed. Because of these expenditures, the American government chose to start producing paper bills for money. With its landmark ruling in 1965, the U.S. Supreme Court affirmed that all American government issued money, including coins and bills, was legal tender. This meant that it had to be taken in payment of debts by every party within the U.S. They similarly ruled that foreign-issued money is not acceptable for forms of payments.

This Supreme Court ruling did not completely settle the issue once and for all. In 2002, the long simmering topic on the issue of currency rose to the forefront of policy debate once again. It was the introducing of the Legal Tender Modernization Act within the U.S. House of Representatives that set it off once again. Besides various other provisos, the act insisted on the termination in circulation of the penny.

Those in favor of the bill under discussion argued that pennies were worthless as a currency since they could not be utilized in most purchases or with vending machines. They cost significantly more than their face value to make and circulate and depend on heavy metal polluting industries in mining both zinc and copper. Despite its public interest, this bill never moved forward into the Congress. Rather it died a slow death for lack of interest and sponsors following the termination of that year's lawmaking session.

Among the great debates for the early years of the 21st century, the Europeans adopting the Euro took monetary center stage. A great number of nations had century's long association with their proprietary and historical national currencies. The switch over to such a common currency format angered the fearful nationalists living within Europe. Around 20 nations eventually joined this new Euro zone and replaced their beloved old currencies with the euro. Most significantly, the U.K., Sweden, and Denmark refused to join and gained exemptions from the common currency requirements and mandate, electing to hold on to their own national currencies instead.

Liabilities

Where a business is concerned, liabilities prove to be amounts of money that are owed by the company at any given point. These liabilities are displayed on the firm's balance sheet. They are commonly listed as items payable, or simply as payables.

There are two types of liabilities. These are longer term liabilities and shorter term liabilities. Long term liabilities turn out to be business obligations that last for greater than the period of a single year. Mortgages payable and loans payable are included in this category.

Short term liabilities represent business obligations that will be paid in less than a year. There are many different kinds of short term liabilities. They include all of the items detailed below.

Payroll taxes payable are one of these. They represent sums automatically collected from the employees and put to the side by the employer. They have to be given to the IRS and any state taxing agencies at the pre determined time.

Sales taxes payable are another short term liability. The business collects them from its customers when sales are made. They hold them until it is time to give them to the proper revenue collecting department within the state.

Mortgages and loans payable are another short term liability. These represent payments made every month on mortgages and loans. They are not large single payments or the total amount of a loan that is eventually owed, but instead represent recurring monthly obligations.

Liabilities for individuals are another type of liabilities altogether. They also represent money that has to be paid out. For people, they are debts owed, as well as monthly cash flow that goes out of the individual's accounts.

Liabilities and assets are the opposites of each other, yet people often get them confused. While assets are things that contribute positive cash flow to a person's finances, liabilities are those that create negative cash flow, or money that leaves an individual's accounts every month. For example, a house that an individual owes money on and makes monthly payments on is a liability, not an asset. The house takes money from the person in the form of monthly mortgage payments each month. For a house to be an asset, it would have to be completely paid off. Even still, if monthly taxes and insurance payments are being made, then technically it would still be a liability. Houses can only be assets really and truly when they are rented out and the rental income that a person receives is greater than all of the expenses associated with the house every month, including any mortgage payments, taxes, insurance, upkeep, and property management fees. When the net result of a property is money coming in, then it is an asset and not a liability.

Lien

A lien is a claim on one individual's property by another person or entity. The party that holds the lien is able to recover the property if a debtor will not follow through with making payments. There are also other circumstances in which liens would allow the lien holder to take the property. Mortgages on houses or buildings prove to be one kind these. Vehicle loans for a business or individual represent other types that are put on the value of the vehicle. When the obligation is paid off, the lien becomes discharged.

Before individuals are able to receive their money after the sale of an asset like a car or house, the lien must be paid off first. With a vehicle, this means that the lender will not send out the title until they receive complete repayment of the principal.

The majority of liens allow for the individuals or businesses to utilize the property as they are paying it. There are scenarios where the lender or creditor physically holds the property while the borrower is making payments. These are a part of bankruptcy procedures as well because they are secured loans with debt repayment rules that have to be addressed in a case.

While there are a number of different types of liens, the most typical one is on a vehicle. Individuals buy a car from the dealer. The bank loans the money and secures the loan. They do this by placing a vehicle lien which allows them to hold on to the automobile's title. The lender files a UCC-1 form to record this. So long as the debtor continues to make payments, the loan will be paid off finally. The bank would then release to the individual the title.

If the individuals stop making their payments, the bank is able to take possession of the vehicle back while still holding the title. If the vehicle owners choose to sell the automobile when they still owe principal, they must clear the bank loan in order to obtain the title. Without the title, a person can not sell the vehicle.

There are a variety of different types of liens in the world. Consensual ones are those which individuals voluntarily accept when they buy something. Non consensual ones are also known as statutory. These come from a court process where an entity places a lien on assets because bills have not been paid. Three of these are fairly common.

A tax lien occurs when individuals do not pay local, state, or federal income taxes. These are put on the offender's property. A judgment lien comes as a result of a case in a small claims court. When a court gives a judgment to one party, the offending party might refuse to pay. In this case the court will place a judgment lien on the offender's property.

A mechanic or contractor lien happens when a contractor performs a job for a home owner. If the owner refuses to pay, the contractor can ask a court to place a lien on the property in question. This would have to be paid off along with other security interests before the property owner is able to sell.

Living Wage

Living Wage refers to an income which would permit the people who earn them to be able to provide for sufficient food, shelter, and other important needs for their livelihood. In order for this wage to be sufficient to sustain an individual and/or family, it has to be high enough that the spending on housing does not exceed 30 percent of the total. The ideal with such a wage is for the workers to be capable of bringing home enough income to maintain an acceptable living standard.

Interestingly enough, the concept for a Living Wage enjoys both proponents and detractors. The critics maintain that enforcing such a livable wage sets a new wage floor that ultimately hurts the overall economy. This argument claims that corporations and small companies will decide to hire fewer employees with these greater amounts of payroll. Such a response would likely lead to a greater unemployment rate. In the end, the argument states that fewer people would be allowed to work for this new wage. Meanwhile those people who are still willing to work for a wage (less than the livable one) will not have job opportunities any more.

Those who support the concept of Living Wage instead suggest that employees who benefit from the higher income will work harder for the firm. This is partly based on the concept that satisfied employees will change companies less frequently. It would lower the costly training and recruiting expenses of companies. A higher wage should similarly increase company morale. Workers wither greater morale tend to enjoy greater productivity. The end beneficiary of the livable wage proves to be the corporation that ultimately gains from better output of its workers.

Part of what makes a living wage confusing is the fact that there are now a number of different definitions for this concept. These also vary by nation as well. For example, in countries like Switzerland and Great Britain, the term concerns a person who is employed for 40 hours per week and has no additional income. In these realms, such an individual ought to be able to afford a reasonable quality of life to include shelter, food, transportation, utilities, a minimum amount of recreation, and quality health care.

In the U.K. capital city London, the GLA Greater London Authority defines

Living Wage as at least 60 percent of the median income plus an extra 15 percent for any unforeseen circumstances. As a tangible example, if the average London area salary amounted to 50,000 British pounds, then the livable wage by their definition would be 30,000 pounds plus another 4,500 pounds for unforeseen emergencies to equal 34,500 pounds in total.

More generally, others define livable wages as those necessary to secure all basic needs for a decent and safe standard of living in a given community. This amount could vary widely from one locality to another based on the costs of living. Activists of the living wage cause have expanded this basic definition to include the amount which equates to the poverty line applicable for a family of four people. This would be sufficient to obtain shelter, food, health care, clothing, transportation, and other daily needs commiserate with life in the modern world.

A more generous definition for Living Wage comes from the Seattle-based Alliance for A Just Society. They define the concept as the amount necessary to cover child care, medical care, housing, education, transportation, food, and pension costs (retirement contributions). They then add on an additional ten percent of that figure to cover savings and debt payoff.

It is easy but wrong to confuse the ideas of minimum wage and livable wage. While a minimum wage is enacted by a national government's policies, laws, and regulations, it is generally insufficient to cover the basic costs and needs of life in society. It forces families to fall back on governmental assistance for the necessities they cannot afford on their own otherwise. Where livable wages have been adopted, this has occurred on a municipal governmental and jurisdictional level. Some places and campaigns have gone a step further and pushed for the idea of a family wage sufficient to support a family.

Local Money

Local Money is money that is created, printed, issued, and traded by an individual community. Communities that are struggling to keep their economies going are in need of a way of boosting the local economic picture. In creating money that can only be utilized by individuals and businesses in their own local area, they attempt to address this problem.

In the United States, local money's history originated in the difficult era of the Great Depression. During this decade of the 1930's, banks were failing in numbers not seen before. This created a real shortage of currency and loans in local communities and towns. Individuals and businesses worked together to find a solution to the problem. They teamed up and created their own currencies that became known as Scrip. Utilizing this newly created local Scrip, trade and exchange continued to go on even with a shortage of banks and hard currency in the smaller towns throughout America.

Today's local money concept has made a comeback in the wake of the financial crisis and the Great Recession. Businesses began working with area banks to come up with their own local currency that could be purchased and issued to consumers in the area. In communities where local money has arisen again, a great number of businesses have signed on to the idea and consented to taking payment in the bills of this localized currency money. This is necessary in order for area consumers to feel compelled to obtain the local money in the first place.

The way that local money works in practice today is interesting. The currency is printed up and then offered by area banks in a participating community. The currency is then sold at a significant discount to its actual value. For example, $100 local money could be sold by area banks for only $95 United States dollars. The $100 local money can then by spent by the consumer at its full value in any business that takes the local money as a method of payment.

Already, over a dozen area communities throughout the U.S. have created their own local money currencies that are being honored on a fairly large scale. Not only is this helping out area businesses by keeping the locally earned paychecks in the communities, but since the currencies are sold at a five to ten percent discount to dollars, it allows struggling workers and families to stretch their incomes by using them. In communities that honor local money, they can be utilized to pay for groceries, gasoline, and even Yoga classes, as examples. Among the more successful and widely accepted local monies these days are the Ithaca Hours of Ithaca, New York; the BerkShares in Western Massachusetts; and the Detroit Cheers in Detroit, Illinois.

The BerkShares for Western Massachusetts are a model case study of successful local money. They can be purchased from twelve banks throughout the area. BerkShares are accepted at in excess of three hundred seventy different businesses in the region. As the largest local money network in the U.S, the BerkShares have so far circulated almost two and a half million dollars. Successes like these have encouraged other communities like South Bend, Indiana to begin creating their own local currency.

Maturity

In the world of business and finance, maturity stands for the last payment date of either a loan or some other form of financial instrument. It is also known as the maturity date. On this maturity date, both the outstanding principal and any remaining associated interest are owed and expected to be rendered for final payment. If they are not paid on the maturity date, such loans or instruments are considered to be in default.

A fixed maturity pertains to a kind of financial instrument where the loan will have to be paid back on a pre set date. Included in fixed maturity instruments are variable rate loans and fixed interest rate loans or other kinds of debt instruments. Besides these, redeemable preferred shares of company stocks fall under this category of fixed maturity instruments. The key to fixed maturities is that they must have a particular maturity date spelled out in their terms. This maturity date is much like a redemption date.

Other instruments do not come with a set fixed maturity date. These kinds of loans go on indefinitely, until the point that a lender and borrower get together and agree on the loan being paid down. These instruments and loans are sometimes referred to as perpetual stocks. Other financial instruments may include a range of potential dates of maturity. These types of stocks may be repaid at any time that suits the borrower, so long as it is within the time range that is provided to them.

Another form of maturity is the serial maturity. Serial maturities mostly pertain to bonds that companies issue to borrow money for a variety of purposes, including expansion into new markets or developing and marketing new products. With serial maturities, all of the bonds are actually issued at one time. Their classes describe the various redemption dates on them, which are generally staggered away from each other.

Maturity is also used by financial news media to discuss securities that have maturities, such as bonds themselves. This abbreviation for these kinds of investments is commonplace. They might claim that the yields declined on twenty year maturities. This would mean that bond prices which are due to reach full maturity in twenty years rose while their actual yields fell, since bond prices move inversely to the direction of their associated yields.

All types of bonds may be referred to using this short hand form of calling them maturities. This could include corporate bonds, Federal Treasury bonds, and also local government municipal bonds. All of these bonds have specific dates of maturity on which they will repay their principal. Preferred stocks also could be thought of as maturities, since they similarly possess set dates on which they are redeemed. They are not commonly referred to by this abbreviation though.

Money Supply

Where business and economics are concerned, the money supply proves to be the complete quantity of money that is available throughout the economy at any given moment in time. Money can be defined in a few different ways. The commonly accepted definitions are comprised of both circulating currency and demand deposits. Demand deposits are the assets of depositors in banks that are easy for them to access, such as checking accounts.

The statistical data on money supply is recorded and made available to the public by the government. In some countries, the central bank publishes such information. Analysts are always interested in any changes to the money supply total, since it has great impacts on inflation levels, prices, and the business cycle.

There are now several different measurements of money supply published within the U.S. These range from narrow to broad money supply totals. While narrower calculations only measure the most liquid of assets that are easy to spend, such as currency itself and checking account deposits, other broader measures include assets that are not so liquid, such as certificates of deposit.

The MB is the complete monetary base as it pertains to all currency. It proves to be the money supply figure that is the most liquid. M1 is the measure that leaves out bank reserves. M2 is the measurement that is given as the main economic indicator in figuring how high inflation will become. Both money and its near substitutes are included in this category. M3 used to be the main figure for money supply in the Untied States, until the Fed elected not to release it any longer after 2006. It included the M2 measure plus longer term deposits.

Inflation commonly results from changes to the money supply. The evidence demonstrates the direct correlation between the growth of the money supply and longer term rising prices. This is particularly the case when the money supply increase is rapid within an economy.

The latest example of how the growth of the money supply can ruin a currency and destroy an economy is demonstrated by Zimbabwe. This African country witnessed dramatic increases in the national money supply and then became a victim of hyperinflation, or a dramatic gain in prices. Because of this, the money supply has to be responsibly controlled and overseen.

The money supply is actually controlled through monetary policy. Central banks such as the Fed determine the money supply in part through their reserve ratios that they make banks observe with percent of deposits kept on hand. They can also adjust it with the interest rates that they set for the country.

Many critics have pointed to the rapid growth in the money supply of U.S. dollars in the years of the financial crisis and the Great Recession as dangerous. From the years of 2007-2010, the dollar money supply has been grown by in excess of three hundred percent. At the same time, the economy has a whole has barely grown. This is the consummate recipe for inflation, and many economists have suggested that you will see high inflation, and potentially even hyperinflation, within the United States in the next several years as a direct result.

Monopoly

Monopolies refer to markets where a single producer or supplier controls all or nearly all of the market. This means that they have the ability to set prices for the good or service they produce. For there to be a true monopoly, there can not be any near substitutes for the product in question. The term monopoly has also come to represent the company which dominates the market of the good or service. Monopolist is another better name for the supplier who controls the market.

When a monopoly exists, there is no competition in the price of the good or service. The monopolist is able to set the price. They will usually choose to make it as high as the market will bear.

Monopolies usually occur because there are particular factors that prevent other companies from competing effectively against the monopolist. These factors are called barriers to entry. There are a number of different barriers to entry which can cause a monopoly to arise.

Sometimes a company exclusively owns a critical resource that companies need to produce the product. This can help it to become a monopoly. Exclusive knowledge of a process to make something would also count as sole ownership of a critical resource. This is what makes pharmaceutical companies monopolies in various types of medicine which they develop and first release.

Government protected ideas can also create monopolies. This can exist in the form of copyrights and patents. In these protections, the government guarantees these companies a minimum period of time to produce the goods or services without any competition. This creates a temporary monopoly until the intellectual property protection expires.

Markets where a good or service is new typically see these types of monopolies. Governments justify copyrights and patents as the means to encourage invention and innovation. Without this temporary protection, many companies would not invest resources needed to create new inventions and products.

A related monopoly is a government franchise. Governments create these types of monopolies when they give the exclusive ability to operate in an industry to a single business. This could happen with a business that is owned by the government or a private company. Train operators and mail delivery companies like the postal service are good examples of this type of government franchise.

Natural monopolies sometimes arise on their own without government help or intervention. This is most often the case when the costs are lower for a single company to service the whole market. Numerous smaller companies competing against each other could actually raise costs and prices in these instances.

Some companies have limitless economies of scale. This means that they are so large and powerful in an industry that no new players could compete with their prices. This could be because the costs to enter the industry are so high that no one will bother. They also represent natural monopolies. There are a number of technology infrastructure companies in this position. Some of the more common industries where these types of natural monopolies occur include telephone operators, Internet service, and cable television providers.

It is not always clear if a company possess a monopoly in a given industry. Some people consider certain brands to be monopolies because of how popular they are. This is true even when they do not control all of the product market share.

The Coca Cola Company has a monopoly on producing the soft drink Coke. This is not the only soft drink on the market, but there is no exact substitute for it. Even though rivals Pepsi Cola and Dr Pepper Snapple Group control a large share of the soft drink market, neither of them produces Coke. This is why the debate for monopolies continues to rage on about what constitutes a close substitute. Anti-monopoly regulators constantly wrestle with the question.

Mortgage

Mortgages are loans made on commercial or residential properties. They commonly use the house or the property itself as collateral. These mortgages are paid off in monthly installments over the course of a pre determined amount of time. Mortgages commonly come in fifteen, twenty, and thirty year periods, though both longer ones and shorter ones are available.

A variety of differing mortgages exist. All of them have their own terms and conditions that translate into advantages and disadvantages. Among the various mortgage types are fixed rate mortgages, adjustable rate mortgages, and balloon payment mortgages.

The most common kinds or mortgages, especially for first time home buyers, prove to be fixed rate mortgages. This is the case because they are both simple to understand and extremely stable. With such a mortgage, the regular monthly payments will be the same during the entire life of the loan. This makes them very predictable and manageable. Fixed rate mortgages have the advantages of protection against inflation, since the interest rate is locked in and can not go up with the floating interest rates. They allow for longer term planning. They come with very low risk, since you are always aware of both the payment and interest rate.

Adjustable rate mortgages, also known as ARM's, have become more popular since they begin with lower, more manageable interest rates that result in a lower initial monthly payment. The downside to them is that the interest rate can and likely will go up and down in the loan's life time. Factors to consider with ARM's are the adjustment periods, the indexes and margins, and the caps ceilings, and floors. The adjustment period is the one in which the interest rate is allowed to reset, commonly starting anywhere from six months to ten years after the mortgage begins.

The interest rates change based on the index and margin. The interest rates are actually based on an index that is published, whether it is the London Interbank Offered Rate, or LIBOR, or the U.S. Constant Maturity Treasury, or CMT. The margin is added to this index to determine the total new interest rate on your mortgage. The amount that these ARM rates are capable of going up or down in a single adjustment period and for the life of the loan is called a cap, a ceiling or a floor.

The third common type of mortgages is balloon reset mortgages. They come with thirty year schedules for repayment, with a caveat. Unless you pay are willing to allow the mortgage to reset to then current interest rates at the end of either a five year or seven year term, then your entire balance will be due at this point. This gives you the benefits of the low monthly payment plan as a person with a thirty year loan would have, yet you will have to be willing to pay off the whole mortgage if you do not take the reset option when the term is up. Because of this, many people refer to this type of a mortgage as a two step mortgage.

Mortgage Broker

A mortgage broker is a firm or sole proprietorship that performs a role as an intermediary between banks and businesses or individuals who are looking for mortgage loans. Even though banks have always vended their own mortgage products, mortgage brokers have gradually taken a larger and larger share of the loan originating market as they seek out direct lenders and banks that have the specific products that a customer wants or needs.

Nowadays, sixty-eight percent of all loans begin with mortgage brokers in the United States, making them by far and away the biggest vendors of mortgage products for banks and lenders. The remaining thirty-two percent of loans come from banks own direct marketing efforts and retail branch efforts. Mortgage broker fees are separate from the bank mortgage fees. They are based on the loans' amounts themselves and range from commonly one to three percent of the total loan amount.

Mortgage brokers are mostly regulated in order to make sure that they comply with finance laws and banking rules in the consumer's jurisdiction. This level of regulation does vary per state. Forty-nine of the fifty states have their own laws or boards that regulate mortgage lending within their state's borders. The industry is similarly governed by ten different federal laws that are applied by five federal agencies for enforcement.

Banks find mortgage brokers to be an ideal means of bringing in borrowers who will qualify for a loan. In this way, a mortgage broker acts as a screening agent for a bank. Banks are furthermore able to shift forward a portion of the fraud and foreclosure risks to the loan originators using their contractual legal arrangements with them. In the originating of a loan, a mortgage broker will do the footwork of collecting and processing all of the necessary paper work associated with real estate mortgages.

Mortgage brokers should not be confused with loan officers of a bank. Mortgage brokers are typically state registered and also licensed in order to work as a mortgage broker. This makes them liable personally for any fraud that they commit during the entire life span of the loans in question. Being a mortgage broker comes with professional, legal, and ethical responsibilities that include proper disclosure of mortgage terms to consumers.

Mortgage brokers come with all kinds of experience, as do loan officers, who are employees of banks. While loan officers commonly close more loans than mortgage brokers actually do because of their extensive network of referrals within the bank for which they work, the majority of mortgage brokers make more money than loan officers make. Mortgage brokers generate the lion's share of all loan originations within the country as well.

Mortgage brokers are all represented by the NAMB, which is the acronym for their group the National Association of Mortgage Brokers. The NAMB's mission is to represent the industry of mortgage brokers throughout the U.S. It also offers education, resources to members, and a certification program as well.

Mortgage Insurance

Mortgage Insurance refers to a policy that helps would-be homeowners to buy a house with a smaller amount of down payment than traditional bank mortgages require upfront. It is these large typically 20 percent down payments that keep many people from the American dream of home ownership. Such insurance is also known by its popular acronym MI.

Thanks to private mortgage insurance, individuals are able to buy a house and put down a smaller amount than 20 percent. Most lenders and investors alike will insist on such mortgage insurance on any down payment that amounts to under 20 percent. Such MI gives lenders the peace of mind and financial backing that if a loan falls into foreclosure, they will receive financial compensation. This kind of guarantee helps many (if not most) lenders to work with less than the standard 20 percent down payment in home loan scenarios.

The real world application of such MI happens like this. A home buyer wants to purchase a $200,000 house. He is only able to put down 10 percent, amounting to $20,000, for his down payment. The lender will then get the privately issued mortgage insurance on the remaining $180,000 which is the mortgage amount. This will reduce the lender's total exposure from $180,000 down to $150,000. This is because the MI will cover the top 25 percent to 30 percent of the mortgage amount. In this example, the MI has protected 25 percent, or $30,000 beyond the $20,000 down payment, from any end-losses the lender would take in the event of foreclosure on the house. Meanwhile the monthly premiums will become a part of the monthly mortgage payment amount, added on to the monthly amount due for the mortgage repayment.

There can be no doubt of the clear advantages this offers lenders. Yet home buyers also gain from MI in several important ways. The first of these is that they are able to purchase a house far sooner than they would be able to otherwise if they had to save an entire 20 percent standard down payment up themselves. It also boosts their ultimate buying power since they are no longer required to put down a full 20 percent. It is partially refundable according to a pro-rated schedule of premiums when it is cancelled through selling the house before the mortgage has been paid off.

PMI helps to secure quicker approvals for home buyers. Finally, home buyers gain greater cash flow alternatives and flexibility on money that they do not have to put down at closing and tie up with the purchase of the house.

Most MI policies are allowed by the lender to be cancelled out after the loan balance declines to less than 75 percent to 80 percent of the total value of the house. The associated premiums also can be paid according to flexible means with many policies. Some will allow buyers to pay for part or even the entire premium in an initial lump sum during closing so that the monthly premiums will be lower. In either case, the policy can be cancelled when it is no longer needed or the buyer sells the house and pays off the mortgage in the process.

Some lenders will offer to pay the MI premium on the behalf of the home buyer. This is rarely done for free however. The tradeoff to the home buyer is that the lender will boost either the interest rate throughout the life of the mortgage loan or the fees they assess at closing time. This is why it is so critical to understand what the costs are when a lender offers to cover the premium on private mortgage insurance.

Mutual Funds

Mutual funds prove to be collective investment pools that are managed professionally. They derive their sometimes enormous capitals from the contributions of many different investors. These monies are then invested in a variety of investments and securities comprised of bonds, stocks, other mutual funds, money markets, and commodities like silver and gold.

Mutual funds all have a fund manager. His responsibility is to sell and buy the holdings of the fund according to the guidelines spelled out in the particular mutual fund's prospectus. U.S. regulations require that all mutual funds registered with the governing SEC, or Securities and Exchange Commission, make distributions of practically all income and net gains made from selling securities to the investors minimally once a year. The majority of these mutual funds are furthermore overseen by trustees or boards of directors. Their job is to make certain that the fund is properly managed by its investment adviser for the investors of the funds ultimate good.

There are really a wide variety of different securities that mutual funds are permitted by the SEC to purchase. This is somewhat limited by the objectives spelled out in the prospectus of the fund, which is comprised of a great amount of useful information on the fund and its goals. While cash instruments, stocks, and bonds are the more common types of investments that they purchase, mutual funds might also buy exotic types of investments like forwards, swaps, options, and futures.

The investment objectives of mutual funds explain clearly the types of investments that the fund will purchase. As an example, if a fund's objective claimed that it was attempting to realize capital appreciation through investing in U.S. company stocks regardless of their amount of market capitalization, then it would be a U.S. stock fund that purchased U.S company stocks.

Other mutual funds purchase specific market sectors or different industries. Utilities, technology, and financial service funds are examples of this. Such a fund is called a sector fund or specialty fund. There are also bond funds that purchase different kinds of bonds, like investment grade corporate bonds or high yield junk bonds. They can invest in the bonds issued by government agencies, municipalities, or companies.

They might also be divided up according to whether they purchase long term or short term maturities of bonds. These funds may also buy bonds or stocks of either domestic companies or global companies, or even international companies outside of the United States. Index funds are another type of mutual fund that attempts to match a certain market index's performance over time. The S&P 500 index is an example of one on which index mutual funds are based. With this type of index fund, the mutual fund would find derivatives based on the S&P 500 stock index futures so that they could match the index's performance as identically as possible.

To help investors better understand the type of fund that they are getting into, the SEC came out with a particular name rule in the 40' Act that makes funds actually invest in minimally eighty percent of securities that actually match up with their name. So a fund called the New York Tax Free Bond Fund would have to use eighty percent or more of its funds to purchase investments of tax free bonds that New York State and its various agencies issued.

Overdraft

An Overdraft refers to the extension of credit where a bank or other lending institution allows for debits to be paid after an account has hit zero dollars. Thanks to these overdrafts, individuals are able to keep drawing down the account value below zero, although there is no money left in it or an insufficient amount to resolve the withdrawal. Another layman's definition of this term is when the bank permits its clients to borrow a given sum of money.

When individuals possess an account with overdraft facilities, the bank will courtesy cover any checks that will put it into overdraft instead of returning them unpaid (bouncing them back to the check depositor). Naturally the outstanding overdrawn balance will have interest charged on it, as with any loan. Typically such interest rates prove to be far lower than those offered by credit cards though. Sometimes there may be other fees for utilizing the overdraft protection. This would decrease the overdraft protection amount available. Some of these could be per withdrawal or per check insufficient funds assessed fees.

Such overdrafts on money market savings accounts, regular savings accounts, and checking accounts happen when the customers do not keep sufficient funds within this account to cover the incidents such as check and ATM withdrawal transactions. In order for it to equal an overdraft, the bank will have to be willing to process and cover the transaction regardless of the shortfall of funds.

Many banks will pay overdrafts on four kinds of banking transactions. These include recurring transactions of debt cards, checks and related transactions that rely on the account number, online banking transfers and payments, and auto bill payments.

Banks might decide to utilize their own corporate funds in order to pay a client overdraft. They might also have customers link the overdraft on to one of their credit cards. When banks deploy their own money in order to pay an overdraft, then this does not usually impact a client's credit score. As credit cards are utilized to cover overdrafts, this could increase the client debt to the amount where the credit score became negatively impacted.

This does not directly result from checking account overdrafts however.

The problem comes when the overdrafts do not become repaid in a prearranged time frame. The bank might opt to hand over the account into the hands of a collection agency. Such a collection activity might negatively impact the credit score if it becomes reportable to any or all of the three primary credit agency bureaus of TransUnion, Experian, or Equifax. This comes down to how the collection agency reports its accounts to the agencies. It will determine whether the overdraft protection on a checking account shows up as a problem or not.

Such Overdraft protection will deliver a useful tool to help manage the checking account on a day to day basis. For example, a person might easily forget that they drew out money for a Starbucks or Costa Coffee run. The overdraft protection will make sure that the ATM is not turned down or that the ATM Debit card purchase does not get rejected at the merchant point of sale. Banks will commonly assess an overdraft fee and use this to make money from the convenience they are delivering. This is why such protection should not be too commonly used and over-utilized. Instead it is to be reserved for emergency needs and situations.

Every overdraft protection dollar amount is not equal. Each bank and type of bank account will vary the level of protection they deliver. This could also vary on a case by case basis. When such protection is overused, the bank or other financial institution may simply elect to remove the courtesy off of the bank account. Getting it reactivated after such a penalizing move is never easy.

Paper Assets

Paper assets have three different meanings depending on whether you are discussing business, investments, or fiat currencies. Where business is concerned, paper assets are assets that you can not easily use or change in to cash. These paper assets possess extremely low liquidity, meaning that they are difficult to sell too. The term in this case literally arises from assets that are valuable on paper, or that have a paper only value.

In investments, paper assets mean something entirely different. They refer to assets that are representations of something. Paper assets in investments literally are pieces of paper that define ownership of an asset. Classic examples of investing paper assets prove to be stocks, currencies, bonds, money market accounts, and similar types of investments. For paper assets to have a tangible value, there must be a working financial system in order to back them up and exchange them. In the cases where a financial system collapses, paper assets commonly sharply decline along with it. The majority of Americans have placed an overwhelming percentage of their money in paper assets, and as the Financial Crisis of 2007-2010 showed, this makes them extremely vulnerable to economic calamities.

Paper assets stand apart in contrast to hard assets. Hard assets contain actual value in the nature of the item itself. There are many forms of hard assets, but among the most popular are gold, silver, diamonds, oil, platinum, land, and other such physical holdings. While financial collapses can cause a set back for the value of hard assets, these types of assets almost always hold up far better than do paper assets.

Many people are shocked by the fact that the U.S. dollar is also a paper asset, as are all Fiat currencies in the world except for the Swiss Franc. These paper currencies are no longer backed up by the long running gold standard. Instead, they only have value because their respective issuing governments, as well as the underlying currency users, say that they do. The Swiss Franc is a lonely exception. The Swiss constitution requires that for every four paper or electronic currency Swiss Francs in existence, there must be one Swiss Franc worth of gold in the Swiss National Bank vaults. Since the Swiss only value their gold holdings at around $250 per ounce, and gold has been trading between $1,300 and $1,400 per ounce for some time now, the Swiss actually have a greater gold backing to their currency than one hundred percent.

Paper Investments

Paper investments can be several things. Where businesses are concerned, paper investments turn out to be investments in commercial paper. Commercial paper investments prove to actually be money market instruments that companies and banks sell to raise money. There are many large issuers with good credit who offer these types of paper investments to interested investors. They represent inexpensive other sources of short term funding as opposed to standard bank loans.

Commercial paper investments come with a fixed maturity of from one day to two hundred and seventy days. These types of paper investments are generally regarded as extremely secure, although they are unsecured loans. The companies that take advantage of them are commonly utilizing these short term operating funds for working capital or inventory purchases.

Corporations like to utilize commercial paper because they are able to quickly and effectively raise significant sums of money without having to get involved with costly SEC registration through selling paper investments. This can be done through working with independent dealers, or on their own efforts directly to investors. Institutional buyers commonly prove to be significant buyers of these types of paper investments.

Such notes come with amounts and maturity dates that can be specifically crafted to meet particular needs. The key features of these types of paper investments are that they are of short term maturity, commonly ranging from only three to six months of time. They liquidate on their own, with no action being required by the investing party in question. There is little to no speculation involved in their intended use as well. This gives them an appeal of clarity.

Offering this type of paper investments offers several advantages for the issuer as well. The issuer is able to access cash at rates that are lower than those offered at the bank. Companies taking advantage of commercial paper are able to leave open reserves of borrowing power at their area banks. Finally, they are capable of getting cash on hand which will allow them to benefit from trade creditors who offer special discounts for those who pay for supplies and other needs with cash.

Where traditional investments are concerned, paper investments also prove to be investments whose value is stated on and represented by paper. A number of different kinds of popular investments in the United States qualify as paper investments. These include stocks, bonds, mutual funds, certificates of deposits, and money market accounts. Shares of stock are pieces of paper that relate a certain percentage of ownership in a publicly traded company.

Most any type of investment that does not have a physical component of the investment associated with it is considered a paper investment. Commodities, as well as futures and options on futures that permit you to take delivery of the underlying commodities if you wish, represent examples of investments that are not only paper investments. These types of investments, along with real estate holdings, are considered to be physical, or hard, investments.

Passive Income

Passive income refers to money that, once it is arranged and established, does not require additional work from the person getting it. A variety of different types of passive income exist. Among them are movie, music, book, screenplay, television, and patent royalties. Other samples of passive income include click through income, rental income, and revenue from online advertising.

Activities that lead to passive income have something in common. They usually need a great amount of money, time, or both invested in them upfront to get them started. There are financial means to establishing passive income as well. You could purchase a rental property or choose to invest in a partnership or other form of company where you are a silent partner. The income that you derive from these investment activities is deemed to be passive.

Various other kinds of passive income do not need a great deal of financial investment made in them, but instead require great amounts of effort, time, and even creativity to achieve. More than a year can be required to either build up a popular website that can contribute passive income from advertising or to write a great novel. Making money from such passive income that is actually profit may take longer.

Books are a good example of how long it can take to actually make money from passive income. Publishers generally get to recover all of their printing and promoting costs, as well as any advance monies given to authors, before royalties are created and paid. Books that sell poorly could turn out to pay the author little to nothing.

Websites have a different set of challenges for their creators. There has to be more than simply good content to make money from them. They must similarly rank high in the search engine results for the necessary amount of visitors to find and go to the website. Unless a great number of visitor hits are recorded on a website, the passive income that is generated will be negligible or even none.

People are willing to put in such a huge amount of time with little assurance of results because they know that the passive income generating activity will create money for them around the clock for years to come, if it is successful. This means that passive income money is constantly being made, even when the person is asleep or on vacation. If you are able to get one passive income project up and running well, then you can attempt others. This way, you might hope to develop a few different income streams that result in a significant annual revenue which can even support you.

Many investors believe that passive income is the most superior kind that you can achieve. This is why rental properties can be so popular. Even though they can require a significant amount of maintenance work and tenant management, they can provide substantial income once several such properties are owned and made profitable.

Pension Funds

Pension funds are retirement plans which mandate that an employer must do contributions for the benefit of their employee's future. They contribute such money into a pool of funds. This pool then becomes invested for the employee's benefit. All earnings which the investments make accrue to the workers once they reach retirement.

Besides these mandatory contributions, there are pension plans which have components of voluntary contributions. Pension plans can permit workers to contribute a portion of their wages and income into the investment plan to help prepare for their retirement. It is also customary and encouraged for an employer to match some part of the yearly contributions of the employees. The limitations on this amount which they can contribute by matching funds are set by the Internal Revenue Service or IRS.

Two primary kinds of pension funds exist today. With defined benefit plans, the companies promise their staff will obtain a minimum benefit amount when they retire. These kinds of plans deliver the minimum regardless of how poorly the investment pool that underlies the fund actually performs. This means that the employer will be required to make a particular pension payment guarantee for their retired employees in these cases.

There is a formula that determines the precise amount. It is typically built on the combination of years in service and aggregate earnings. In the cases where the pension plan assets are insufficient to pay out the defined and guaranteed minimum benefits, then it is the firm which will have to make up the balance of the minimum payment.

Such employer sponsored pension plans and pension funds in the United States hail from the decade of the 1870s. At their peak in the roaring 1980s, they amounted to a participation rate of almost 50 percent of the total workers in the private sector. Around 90 percent of all public employees as well as approximately 10 percent of the private ones receive the coverage of this kind of defined benefits plan nowadays.

The second type of pension funds are defined contribution plans. With these, the employing company engages in particular set contributions to the retirement plans of their employees. They typically will match to some degree their employees' contributions to the plan. The ultimate payouts which the staff receive while retired come down to the investment results of the plan. In these cases, the firms which sponsor them do not have additional minimum payout liability after they make their pre-set contributions.

The reason these are so much more popular now is that they prove to be far less costly for employers than do traditional forms of pensions. This is because companies are not backing whatever benefits the funds are unable to produce. More and more private corporations and firms have moved over to this form of plan and have closed out their defined benefit plans. While there are a number of defined contribution plans, the 401(k) plan is the most well-known one. For the benefit of not for profit workers, the equivalent plan turns out to be the 403(b) plan.

When the phrase is utilized, "pension plan" typically refers to these more traditional forms of defined benefit plans. These payouts remain established, controlled, and ultimately funded 100 percent by the sponsoring employer. There are corporations which provide a choice from both plan types. Some will even permit their workers to roll over their 401(k) plan balances to their defined benefit or "pension" plans.

A final version of these is the pay as you go pension plan. Employers set these up themselves. Such plans are entirely funded during the accumulation phase by the workers. They may choose to make either a lump sum contribution (as with an annuity) or regular salary-deducted contributions. Besides these capabilities, such plans prove remarkably similar to other 401(k) plans. One disadvantage to them is that they lack a company matching participation program.

Personal Assets

Personal assets are items of value that belong to an individual. There are many examples of such tangible personal assets. Among these are houses, real estate, cars, and jewelry. Personal assets can also be any other thing with cash value.

When individuals go to a bank or other institution to apply for loans, such personal assets and their values are often considered. These assets are also the bedrock of the formula for net worth for consumers. The value of people's personal assets can be higher than they expect and surprise them as so many different items can be included under this label.

There are many personal assets that are material and easy to measure. These include such financial assets as savings accounts, checking accounts, and retirement accounts. Assets that have a value that can not be easily accessed are also included in the personal assets category. This includes life insurance policies and annuities that have cash values. Other items of value which would be included in a list of personal assets cover such items as antiques, art collections, electronics, personally owned businesses, and other valuable items.

Personal assets can do more than simply help people get loans and count towards net worth. They are also sometimes able to create income for their owners. Bank accounts and savings accounts accrue interest. Holders of real estate are able to lease or rent it out. This brings in rent or lease fees. Individuals who have personal assets should educate themselves in the best practices for managing them so that they are able to increase their total wealth by generating the highest income possible from them.

It is important to keep a careful track of rent or other income obtained from personal assets as the money will be taxable. Income that is not properly reported to the government on the correct tax forms can incur penalties from the Internal Revenue Service.

It is also important to know the value of an individual's personal assets. There are two different methods of learning this. In the first method, individuals examine the item's market value. This is the value for which the asset would sell if a person were to put it straight on the market. Another way to determine the value of these assets is to have a personal asset appraised.

Appraised values can be substantially greater than market values. This is because an appraisal value relies on the possible future price of the item in question. This difference matter significantly, particularly when having an item insured. Individuals generally have to obtain appraised value insurance coverage. This means that they will likely have to pay for a greater amount of insurance.

When properly managed, personal assets can greatly contribute to an individual's personal financial situation. It is also true that these assets can prove to be a liability if they are not well taken care of or managed. Part of managing assets well involves asset allocation.

Financial experts warn against placing all or the majority of personal assets into a single asset type or location. This type of practice causes people to take on additional risk than is prudent. Instead, it is better to spread around an individual's wealth into a variety of different assets so that if one suffers or decreases in value, some of the other assets may offset this by outperforming or increasing in value.

Taking care of personal assets is also an important part of maintaining their value. Individuals can break expensive electronics if they are not careful. Not engaging in proper maintenance for works of art can also lead to their value declining over time.

Ponzi Scheme

Ponzi Schemes prove to be frauds surrounding investments that are related to the pay out of returns to investors in the scheme that are covered using contributions from new investors. The individuals who run Ponzi schemes are able to attract newer investors through boasting of tremendous opportunities that will guarantee terrific investment returns, typically with little to no risk.

With a great number of these Ponzi Schemes, the managers of the scheme concentrate their efforts on constantly bringing in new sums of money in order to be capable of giving out the payments that they promised investors from earlier time periods. Besides this, they utilize the new money for their own personal expenses. Rarely does any energy actually go into real investment opportunities and strategies.

Ponzi schemes always fail at some point in time. This eventually happens since there are no real earnings to distribute. Because of this problem, Ponzi schemes need constant money flowing into them from newer investors in order to survive. As attracting newer investors becomes more challenging, or if a great number of currently involved investors request their money back, then the Ponzi Scheme will likely fall apart.

Ponzi Schemes actually earned their name from a famed early con artist Charles Ponzi. He became famous after he tricked literally thousands of well to do New Englanders into pouring their money into his speculation in postage stamps in the 1920's. The allure of his scheme proved to be hard to resist, since bank accounts were paying only five percent annual returns while he offered investors incredible returns of fifty percent in only ninety days. In the early days, Charles Ponzi really did purchase a small quantity of international mail coupons to support his investment scheme. Before long, he decided to employ the money that came in to cash out earlier investors.

The most successful Ponzi Scheme of all time proved to be the one run by Bernie Madoff. Madoff ran an over thirty year, over thirty billion dollar investment scheme that tricked thousands of investors out of their money. Madoff proved to have a different angle on his Ponzi scheme in that he did not offer his investors who were short term amazing returns. Rather than this, he sent out fake account statements that constantly demonstrated moderate but always positive gains, no matter how turbulent the market proved to be.

Bernie Madoff is presently undergoing a one hundred and fifty year sentence in federal prison for his activities. His investment advisory company began back in 1960 and did not come down until the end of 2008. All during the years that his scheme ran, he served as Vice Chairman of the National Association of Securities Dealers, and even as a member of the board of governors and chairman for the NASDAQ stock market.

The Securities Exchange Commission is ultimately responsible for discovering and prosecuting Ponzi Schemes. They typically utilize emergency actions to freeze assets while they break up the schemes. In 2009 as an example, the SEC actually pursued sixty different Ponzi schemes, the highest profile one of which turned out to be Robert Allen Stanford's $8 billion Ponzi scheme.

Portfolio

In the world of business and finance, a portfolio stands for an investment collection that a person or institution holds. People and other entities put together portfolios in order to diversify their holdings to reduce risk to a manageable level. A number of different kinds of risk are mitigated through the acquisition of a few varying types of assets. A portfolio's assets might be comprised of stocks, options, bonds, bank accounts, gold certificates, warrants, futures contracts, real estate, facilities of production, and other assets that tend to hold their value.

Investment portfolios may be constructed in various ways. Financial entities will commonly do their own careful analysis of investments in putting together a portfolio. Individuals might work with the either financial firms or financial advisors that manage portfolios. Alternatively, they could put together a self directed portfolio through working with a self directed online broker such as TD Ameritrade, eTrade, or Scott Trade.

A whole field of portfolio management has arisen to help with the allocation of investment money. This management pertains to determining the types of assets that are appropriate for an individual's risk tolerance and ultimate goals. Choosing the instruments that will comprise a portfolio has much to do with knowing the kinds of instruments to buy and sell, how many of each to obtain, and the time that is most appropriate to purchase or sell them.

Such decisions are rooted in a measurement for the investments' performance. This usually pertains to risk versus return on investments and anticipated returns of the entire portfolio. With portfolio returns, various types of assets are understood to commonly return amounts of differing ranges. Portfolio management has to factor in an individual investor's own precise situation and desired results as well. There are investors who are more fearful of risk than are other investors. These kinds of investors are termed risk averse. Risk averse portfolios are significantly different in their composition than are typical portfolios.

Mutual funds have evolved the act of portfolio management almost to a science. Their fund managers came up with techniques that allow them to prioritize and ideally set their portfolio holdings. This fund management reduces risk and increases returns to maximum levels. Strategies that these managers have created for running portfolios include designing equally weighted portfolios, price weighted portfolios, capitalization weighted portfolios, and optimal portfolios in which the risk adjusted return proves to be the highest possible.

Well diversified portfolios will contain many different asset classes. These will include far more than just stocks, bonds, and mutual funds. They will feature international stocks and bonds to provide diversification away from the U.S. dollar, as well as foreign currencies and hard asset commodities such as real estate investments, and gold and silver holdings.

Portfolio Income

Portfolio income proves to be money that is actually brought in from a group of investments. The portfolio commonly includes all of the various types of investments that an investor owns. These include bonds, stocks, mutual funds, and certificates of deposit. These various financial instruments earn a variety of different types of passive income, such as dividends, interest income, and capital gain distributions. Such portfolio income returns are generated by the holdings of the various investment products in the portfolio.

Portfolio income varies with the types of investments that an investor picks. You as an investor will commonly look at two different factors when assembling a portfolio for portfolio income. These turn out to be the money that the investment itself will produce, which is also known as an investment's return, and the investment's risk level that it contains.

As an example, stocks are frequently deemed to be investments with considerable risk, yet the other side of the risk return equation is that they provide income from a company's dividends, or distribution earnings returned to the shareholders, as well as an increase in the stock price as the stock value gains with time. Certificates of deposit and bonds create interest income that is paid out on the investment that you hold. Still different kinds of investments produce other types of income, although this depends on the characteristics of the investment in question.

To maximize the portfolio income while reducing the amount of risk involved, individuals commonly choose to invest in numerous different kinds of investments. This is known as diversifying your portfolio and portfolio income. This way, you can combine both safer investments that provide lower real returns with riskier investments that offer greater investment returns. Your total collection of investments is the portfolio that makes your portfolio income for you.

This portfolio income is also classified as passive income, or income that does not require you to perform any work in order to make the money. The upfront investment actually creates the income without you having to be actively involved in the money making process. This stands in contrast to incomes that are earned through active involvement, or active income that you must expend both energy and time to create.

The ultimate goal for you with your portfolio income will probably be to build up enough of it that you are capable of living off of only the income that the portfolio generates. Once this point is reached, you would be able to not receive a payroll check any longer. Instead, you would support yourself in retirement from the dividends, interest, and capital gains created by the investments in the form of portfolio income. The best and safest way to do this is to only draw on the portfolio income itself, without drawing down the original principal.

By not touching the investment principal, you allow your portfolio and resulting portfolio income to build up over time. If you do not take out the portfolio income, then the total value of the portfolio will grow faster with time, allowing you to compound your investments for retirement. It is critical to have enough money saved for retirement that you do not need to take out this principal to support yourself. Sufficient portfolio income should be generated to cover the monthly retirement expenses. In this way, you will not be reducing your principal and risking the very real danger of your portfolio running out of money while you are still alive to need it.

Power of Attorney

A power of attorney is an agreement in writing that grants another individual the authority to make some choices if the grantor is not available. This person who receives the power does not have to be an attorney. Attorneys are typically only involved in drafting up or potentially witnessing such an agreement. The phrase comes from an individual receiving status as an agent or attorney in fact.

When people implement such a power of attorney they do not lose the ability to make their own decisions. Instead they are allowing another individual to act for them in matters specified within the written text. This can be very helpful if people are out of the country or in the hospital as an example. Someone else with this authority would be able to cash checks at the bank or pay bills on their behalf. It is simply a matter of sharing power with another person. The agent is only carrying out the grantor's wishes, not actually making choices for them, so long as they are coherent and mentally capable.

People who will be out of town for an extended period of time might find these arrangements particularly useful. With a power of attorney, the agent could carry out major decisions such as selling cars or other personal assets. The Internet has eliminated the need for some of these functions as computers and mobile devices make it possible for people to buy and sell stocks and handle many financial transactions from anywhere they have an online connection. There are still cases where a transaction will require an in person agent to handle them.

There is also a special kind of power of attorney that is used by individuals who lose their ability to handle decisions for their personal financial affairs. This is known as a durable power of attorney. In this case, the word durable refers to the ability of the agent to make the choices on the grantor's behalf when he or she can not mentally do them. This type of arrangement grants the agent the legal authority and responsibility to make the best possible physical and financial decisions for the grantor.

It means that the agent is able to spend the individual's money as appropriate, cash checks, deposit checks, and even withdraw money from the personal bank accounts. The agent further gains the authority to sign contracts, sell personal property, take legal actions, and file and follow up on insurance claims.

When people decide to enter a durable power of attorney arrangement, a notary public or lawyer should witness the document before they sign and execute it. If such individuals need to have a durable agreement established and are not mentally able to do it, courts can do this for them as they deem necessary.

Agents who become appointed to this position are expected to keep correct and segregated records on each transaction they perform. The records must also be easily available at all times. When the individual dies, his or her power of attorney becomes null and void. The will is responsible for the dispensation of the deceased person's estate.

Powers of attorney can be rescinded. If individuals feel unhappy in the ways that their agent is managing their personal affairs, they can simply revoke the authority back at any point. It is always wise for people to choose an individual to be agent whom they know and implicitly trust.

Prime Rate

The Prime Rate is the most typically utilized shorter term interest rate for the United State banking system. All kinds of lending institutions in the United States employ this U.S. benchmark interest rate as a basis or index rate to price their medium term to short term loans and products. This includes credit unions, thrifts, savings and loans, and commercial banks.

This makes the Prime Rate consistent around the country as banks strive to be competitive and profitable in their lending rates which they provide to both consumers and businesses. A universal rate like this simplifies the task for businesses and consumers as they shop around comparable loan products that competing banks offer. Every state in the country does not maintain its own benchmark rate. This makes a California Prime or New York Prime identical to the U.S. Prime.

Commercial and other banks charge this benchmark rate to their best customers. These are those clients who have the best credit ratings and loan history with the bank. Most of the time banks' best clients are made up of large companies.

The prime interest rate is also known as the prime lending rate. Banks typically base it on the Federal Reserve's federal funds rate. This is actually the rate that banks loan money to each other for overnight purposes. Retail customers also need to be aware of the prime lending rate. It directly impacts the lending rates that they can access for personal and small business loans as well as for home mortgages.

The federal government and Federal Reserve Bank do not set the prime lending rates. The individual banks set it. They then utilize this base rate or reference rate to set the prices for a great number of loans such as credit card loans and small business loans.

The Federal Reserve Board releases a statistics called "Selected Interest Rates." This is their survey of the prime interest rate as the majority of the twenty-five biggest banks set it. It is this publication which reveals the Prime Rate periodically. This is why the Federal Reserve does not directly set this important benchmark rate. The banks more or less base it on the target level of the federal funds rate that the Federal Open Market Committee sets and changes at their monthly meetings.

Different banks adjust their prime lending rate at the same time. The point where they change it is generally when the Federal Open Market Committee adjusts their own important Fed Funds Rate. Many publications refer to this periodically changing reference rate as the Wall Street Prime Rate.

A great number of consumer loans as well as commercial loans and credit card rates find their basis in the prime lending rate. Among these are car loans, home equity loans, personal and home lines of credit, and various kinds of personal loans.

The rates above the prime lending rate that banks charge their less then prime (or subprime) customers depend on the credit worthiness of the borrower in question. The banks attempt to correctly ascertain the risk of default for the borrower. For the best credit customers who have lower chances of defaulting, banks can afford to assess them a lower interest rate than others. Customers with higher chances of defaulting on their loans pay larger interest rates because of the risk associated with their loans not being repaid.

As of June 15, 2016, the Federal Open Market Committee voted to maintain its target fed funds rate in a range of from .25% to .5%. As a result of this, the U.S. prime lending rate stayed at 3.5%. Once per month the Federal Reserve committee meets to determine if they will change the fed funds rate.

Principal

Principal has several different meanings. It most commonly pertains to the initial amount of money that a person either invests or borrows with a loan. A secondary meaning has to do with a bond and its face value. Sometimes the word pertains to the owners of a company or the main participants in any type of transaction.

Where borrowing is concerned, this term relates to the upfront amount of any loan. It also is utilized to describe original amounts which the individuals still owe on the loan in question. Looking at a clear example always helps to clarify the concept. When people obtain a $100,000 mortgage, this Principal is the same $100,000. As the individuals pay down $60,000 of this amount, the remainder of $40,000 that is left to pay off is similarly referred to as Principal.

It is the original Principal that decides how much interest borrowers will pay. If borrowers take out a loan with an initial amount equaling $20,000 that comes with a yearly interest rate at seven percent, then they would be required to pay $1,400 in annual interest for each year that the loan remains open. As borrowers pay the monthly payments to the loan servicer, the interest charges for the month will first be paid off. What remains goes toward the initial amount which the individuals borrowed. Paying down this original amount borrowed remains the only means of lowering the interest amount that accrues on a monthly basis.

Another form of mortgage that operates differently has the name of zero principal mortgages. Bankers think of these as interest-only loans. They represent a unique form of financing where the routine monthly payments of the borrower only apply to the loan's interest. This means that the initial loan amount never gets paid down unless the borrower makes extra payments. It also translates to no equity building up in the property which backs the mortgage loan.

Because of this, financial advisors will typically not recommend these types of mortgages to home buyers as they are rarely in the true interest of the purchaser. Despite this fairly obvious assessment, there are a few unusual cases when they could work out for certain people. When a home buyer is starting out on a career path that pays very little initially but will later on earn substantially more in the not too distant future, it could be worthwhile to lock in the home price now while it is lower. Once the income increases apace, the borrowers always have the ability to refinance into a more traditional mortgage which would cover payments on the initial amounts borrowed as well.

Another scenario where these loans make sense relates to unusual and fantastic opportunities for a particular real estate investment deal. When huge returns on investment dollars can be anticipated, it is practical to go with these mortgage's far lower payments that are interest-only. Meanwhile the borrower can plow the additional monthly payment money savings into the exceptional investment opportunity.

Principal also finds use describing the first initial outlay on an investment. This does not take into consideration any interest that builds up or earnings on the investment. Savers might deposit $20,000 at a bank in a savings account with interest. After a number of years, the balance will grow to $21,500. The principal remains the original $20,000 the savers gave the bank. The additional $1,500 will be called interest or earnings on top of this initial outlay.

It is interesting to note that inflation will not change the nominal value of a loan or financial instrument's principal. Yet the effects of inflation do very much reduce the real value of the initial amount.

Promissory Note

Promissory notes are negotiable instruments that are called notes payable in accounting circles. In such promissory notes, an issuer writes an unlimited promise that he or she will pay a certain amount of money to the payee. This can be set up either on demand of the payee, or at a pre arranged future point in time. Specific terms are always arranged for the repayment of the debt in the promissory note.

Promissory notes are somewhat like IOU's and yet quite different. Unlike an IOU that only agrees that there is a debt in question, promissory notes are made up of a particular promise to pay the debt. In conversational vernacular, loan contract, loan agreement, or loan are often utilized in place of promissory note, even though such terms do not mean the same things legally. While a promissory note does provide proof of a loan in existence, it is not the loan contract. A loan contract instead has all of the conditions and terms of the particular loan arrangement within it.

Promissory notes contain a variety of term elements in them. Among these are the amount of principal, the rate of interest, the parties involved, the repayment terms, the date, and the date of maturity. From time to time, provisions may be included pertaining to the payee's rights should the issuer default. These rights could include the ability to foreclose on the issuer's assets.

A particular type of promissory note is a Demand Promissory note. This specific kind does not come with an exact date of maturity. Instead, it is due when the lender demands repayment. Generally, in these cases lenders only allow several days advance notice before the payment must be made.

Within the U.S., the Article 3 of the Uniform Commercial Code regulates most promissory notes. These negotiable forms of promissory notes are heavily used along with other documents in mortgages that involve financing purchases of real estate properties. When people make loans in between each other, the making and signing of promissory notes are commonly critical for the purposes of record keeping and paying taxes. Businesses also receive capital via the use of promissory notes that are sometimes referred to as commercial papers. These promissory notes became a finance source for the creditors of the firm receiving money.

Promissory notes have functioned like currency that proved to be privately issued in the past. Because of this, such promissory notes that are bearer negotiable have mostly been made illegal, since they represent an alternative to the officially sanctioned currency. Promissory notes go back to well before the 1500's in Western Europe. Tradition claims that the very first one ever signed existed in Milan in 1325. Reference is made to some being issued between Barcelona and Genoa back in 1384, even though we no longer have the promissory notes themselves. The first one that we still have dates back to 1553 where Ginaldo Giovanni Battista Stroxxi issued one that he created in Medina del Campo, Spain against the city of Besancon.

Rollover IRA

An IRA is the acronym for Individual Retirement Account. These accounts represent a form of government-approved and -created savings account for retirement. They have several advantages, the main one of which is the significant tax breaks they receive in tax deferment. This makes them the optimal way to put cash aside towards eventual retirement. It is important to know that IRAs are not investments. Instead they are more like the basket in which individuals maintain their mutual funds, stocks, bonds, and other assets. When one retirement account is transferred to another one, this is known as a Rollover IRA.

Generally people open such a Rollover IRA themselves. There are also a few types which small business owners and the self employed can open. Among the various types of Individual Retirement Accounts in existence are the Roth IRAs, traditional IRAs, SEP IRAs, and SIMPLE IRAs. Not all of these can be accessed by every individual in the U.S. This is to say that every one of them has specific eligibility requirements which revolve around the type of employment and income level. What they do all have in common is the caps on the amount individuals are allowed to contribute every year. They also mostly share steep penalties for withdrawing funds ahead of the government set age of retirement.

The greatest benefit to these accounts lies in their ability for all of the assets within the plan to gain in value while not being taxed by the U.S. Federal government. This means that all income generated by capital gains, dividends, and interest will compound every year with no tax bite. Taxes on the majority of these forms of IRAs only become due as the owners take qualified (or unqualified with a penalty) distributions. There are two different forms of this. With the majority of the IRAs, individuals are able to commit pre-taxed dollars to the account. With Roth IRAs, the dollars are after-taxed, but then no additional taxes on them will be required upon withdrawals at retirement. Using the Rollover IRA concept, individuals can switch from one type of IRA to another.

The Internal Revenue Service strictly limits how much money people can put into such accounts. The majority of individuals who are less than 50 are not permitted to contribute over $5,500 each year as of 2016. These limits become higher once the holders attain an age greater than 50. They call this "catch up contributions," and the limits are typically raised by $1,000 to $1,500 more in this decade immediately before holders reach retirement age.

Practically all individuals are allowed to make contributions each year to a traditional form of IRA. So long as either the holder or spouse earns taxable income and is less than 70 and a half years old, they can participate.

The various kinds of IRAs are important to understand. A ROTH IRA does not provide tax deductions on contributions. There are also income restrictions which in 2016 amounted to under $184,000 for married filing jointly families or $117,000 for single heads of households or those who are married filing separately and not living with their spouses.

Both SEP and SIMPLE IRAs apply to only small business owners and the self employed. Only employers who claim fewer than 100 employees can set up these SIMPLE IRA accounts. Any individual who possesses freelancing income or who owns a business can open an SEP IRA.

While individuals can always withdraw their contributions (and even earnings) at any point once they have deposited them to their IRAs, there are penalties if they are less than 59 and ½ years old. The penalty is an extra 10 percent above the that-year tax bracket of the individuals who take distributions early. The government's point is to discourage people from utilizing their retirement accounts like ATM machines or credit cards.

Roth IRA

A Roth IRA is a particular type of Individual Retirement Account. These Roth IRA's prove to be special retirement plans that are given favorable tax treatment. The tax laws of the United States permit tax reductions on restricted amount savings for retirement accounts.

Roth IRA's are different from other IRA's in several ways. Among the chief of these is that tax breaks are not given on monies that are put into the plan and account with a Roth IRA. Instead, these tax breaks are given out on the money and its investment gains when they are taken out of the account at retirement. This chief appeal of Roth IRA's is that they provide completely tax free income at retirement.

Other Roth IRA benefits over traditional forms of IRA's exist as well. The restrictions placed on the kinds of investments that they are allowed to contain are fewer. You can turn them into gold IRA's and annuity account IRA's. Roth IRA's can also contain all of the usual forms of investments that IRA's contain, such as mutual funds, stocks, bonds, and certificates of deposit. More unusual investments such as real estate, mortgage notes, derivatives, and even franchises are allowed to be purchased with Roth IRA's. These investment choices do depend on the capability and allowance of the Roth IRA trustee, or firm with which the plan is set up. Roth IRA's also permit you to make un-penalized withdrawals of all direct contributions that you make, after the first five years of the account have and plan have passed, which is certainly not the case with traditional IRA's.

These distributions, or withdrawals, are not taxed because they are taxed before the contributions are made. The penalties are waived for principal, as well as interest and earnings in the account, if the distributions are for purchasing a house or for disability or retirement withdrawal uses. If there is not a justified reason for the distribution, then the account earnings and income made above contributions will be taxed.

All IRA's contain specific limits on the dollar amount of contributions that the government permits. This amount changes per year, and is set through the year 2011 now. Presently, you can put $5,000 per year into Roth IRA's. There are income restrictions that govern whether you are allowed to make this full contribution as well. Individuals who make less than $106,000 are permitted to make full Roth IRA contributions, and those who make under $121,000 may make a partial contribution. Married couples who file together are allowed to earn less than $167,000 to make their full contribution to the Roth IRA, while those who make under $177,000 can do a partial contribution.

Roth IRA conversions from traditional IRA's have been allowed by the IRA in the past, although with certain income restrictions. Beginning in 2010, this policy changed. Now the IRS permits any persons, regardless of how much money that they make, to convert their traditional IRA's into Roth IRA's.

Royalties

Royalties are payments which owners receive in exchange for the use of their property. This most typically covers natural resources, franchises, patents, and copyrighted works. Royalty payments go to the property in question's legal owner. Individuals who want to utilize the owners' patents, property, franchise, natural resources, or copyrighted works will do so with the intention of creating a revenue stream or realizing a lump sum income. Royalties are typically intended to provide compensation for the licensing of the asset. As such, these arrangements become legally binding.

Much of the time, these royalties are stated in percentage of revenue terms. They can also be arranged to fit a particular scenario or environment. They are often employed as the vehicle for realizing income in instances where the owner, inventor, or natural resource holder wishes to sell the product in question in exchange for payments against future revenues that this activity might create for the third party licensor.

An example of this is Microsoft. The computer software giant earns a royalty from every installation of the internationally standard Windows operating system on almost any computer a manufacturer produces. Such an example relates to creative content, copyrights, and patents.

A royalty could also apply to resources, trade marks, art works, books and published works, copyright materials, franchises, patents, and resource holdings. Even fashion designers are able to charge a royalty to other companies that wish to make use of their designs or names. Authors, production pros, and musical artists also receive this kind of compensation when a firm or individual uses their copyrighted and produced works. Cable and satellite firms pay a royalty to the owner of a television channel so they can offer the most stations in a country.

The oil and gas business is one that is rife with royalties. Companies provide a royalty to a landowner in exchange for permission to gather the natural resources off of their private property. This might amount to so much money per barrel of oil or per cubic foot of natural gas which they extract.

A license agreement is a key component of a royalty. It represents the terms by which the property owner will receive the payments. This clearly and legally explains the restrictions and limitations of the royalty in question. As an example, it would deal with the length of time the agreement will endure, the geographic territorial limitations, and the specific amounts they will pay for the various kinds of products utilized or extracted. These types of license agreements are differently and specifically regulated depending on whether the owner of the resource or property in question is a private individual or the government.

A royalty rate represents the specific amount of payment that must be paid for a given service or product. This will naturally depend on the kind of fee the third party is providing. There are a number of different factors involved in a royalty rate. Among the most frequently cited examples are alternative option availability, rights' exclusivity, the relevant risks involved, technological sustainability, structure of the market demand, and scope of the innovation which the service or product offers.

These terms should not be confused with a royalty trust unit. Such units provide the holder of the unit with a share of the income which the properties a trust owns actually produce. These royalty trusts acquire ownership stakes in cash flows or general operating concerns. The royalty trust itself will own the cash flow or income which the company is generating. They will then pass through this money to the trust royalty unit holders. Such royalty units have often been viewed as positive and desirable investments since the income which the asset creates only becomes subject to individual tax levels. There is no so-called "double taxation" as common stocks dividends experience (on both the company earning the money and then the person receiving it again).

Self Directed IRA

Self directed IRAs prove to be special kinds of individual retirement accounts. They are different from traditional IRAs because they provide the account holder with a significantly greater variety of investment choices and control over decisions on the account. With these types of IRAs, the owner or an investment advisor makes a variety of investment decisions. They then deliver these instructions to an IRA custodian who executes them.

Federal law allows these types of IRAs to invest in a tremendous range of investment vehicles. It is IRS section 408 that restricts the few categories that are not allowed. The IRS forbids investments of IRA funds in life insurance and collectibles such as rugs, art, gems, etc. It does allow a wide range of investment choices that cover most anything else.

Self directed IRAs may purchase real estate, mortgages and trust deeds, energy investments, gold and other precious metals in bullion form, privately held stock, privately owned LLCs and Limited Partnerships, and corporate debt or promissory notes. When accounts such as these are opened primarily to purchase precious metals bullion, they are typically known by the name of their primary metal in which they invest.

These Precious Metals IRAs can be called Gold IRAs, Silver IRAs, Platinum IRAs, and Palladium IRAs. Such self directed IRAs can even purchase franchises such as Subway or Timothy Horton. All of these different investment choices allow for superior and broad based asset diversification of investors' retirement funds.

These types of IRAs also provide all of the usual benefits which are commonly associated with Traditional IRAs. Money saved in these plans is contributed on a tax free or tax deferred basis. No taxes will be paid on either the money deposited, or the gains made on these investments within the account, until they are withdrawn at retirement or under early withdrawal rules and limitations. Self directed IRAs are still subject to the same yearly maximum contribution limits of $5,500 in 2016. They allow for larger contributions of $6,500 to be made as catch up once the account holders reach age 50.

Early withdrawals from these IRAs as with traditional ones are penalized. It is often more advantageous to take a loan against the value of the IRA rather than suffer the financial consequences of early withdrawal. When loans are taken, there is no penalty. A repayment plan is established to put the borrowed funds back in the account in installments. Loans can be approved for a variety of expenses, such as home purchase, educational needs, or health care related expenses.

When an actual early withdrawal is taken, two penalties are assessed. First the money in the account is taxed as ordinarily earned income. Next a 10% penalty is levied by the IRS on all monies which the owner early withdraws.

These types of IRAs do have some limitations. The custodian must physically hold all assets in the account. This means that the account owners are not allowed to keep their real estate or mortgage deeds, stock certificates, or precious metals bullion at home in a safe. There have been offers made by some companies to help investors become their own IRA custodian by forming a special LLC company. This is a gray area which the IRS has not yet come down on with a hard ruling. In the future, they are likely to rule that investors absolutely can not be a custodian for their own gold, silver, platinum, or palladium bullion using either a safe deposit box or a home based safe.

The IRS requires that owners of these accounts begin taking distributions no later than at age 70. They can start withdrawing them as retirement funds at 59 ½ if they wish to begin using the money earlier.

SEP IRA

SEP IRAs are special simplified employee pensions that permit employers to contribute money to the retirement plans of their employees. If individuals are self employed, they may also set up and fund one of these accounts for their own benefit. These plans compare favorably to the more popular and utilized 401(k) plan. SEPs offer greater contribution amount limits. They are also much less complicated to establish and maintain than are the 401(k)s.

Any type of employer is allowed to create an SEP IRA. This means that businesses which are not incorporated, partnerships, and sole proprietorships can all work with and utilize them. Even self employed individuals who are employed elsewhere as well (with retirement plans at their other workplace) can make their own SEP.

SEP IRAs offer several advantages to owners and contributors. They provide significant tax benefits for employees and employers. Employer contributions give tax deductions to the employer during the tax year in which they make the contribution. Self employed individuals also can take this tax deduction for themselves. SEPs are also popular because they do not require any annual paperwork to be filed with the IRS. The paperwork that creates these accounts also offers the plus of being simple and minimal.

Individuals can make contributions for SEP IRAs in the year after the contribution applies. Deadlines for these contributions may also be stretched to the tax return due date. As far as establishing these accounts goes, deadlines are for the tax return due date and any extension that the IRS grants on the taxes.

In general, these accounts have to be opened and all contributions should be made by the April 15th that comes after the year in which the income was attained. Any taxpayers who take an extension on their tax returns to October 15th would receive a similar grace period for opening and funding the SEP IRA.

The contribution amounts for SEPs are quite flexible. No set percentage has to be contributed as with some of the rival retirement accounts like

Keoghs. One could contribute nothing or as much as 25% of his or her income for the year (on as high as a $265,000 income amount). The full contribution for a single individual is not allowed to be greater than $53,000 in the year 2016. This amount contrasts with the typical standard IRA contribution limits of $5,500 for the year 2016.

The SEP limits are also substantially higher than the contribution limits on 401(k)s that come in at $18,000 for 2016 or at $24,000 for those who are at least 50 years old. SEPs do not have any provisions for catch up, as with other forms of IRAs or 401(k)s. Thanks to the higher contribution limits for every given year, this does not usually present a problem for those who are behind on their retirement accounts and want to put in more.

Employers are required to treat all employee contributions equally. This means that they must give the same contribution percentage for each employee who has made at least $600 in the year, who is 21 years or older, and who has worked for the company minimally three out of five prior years.

The only point where contributions to SEP IRAs get complicated centers on maximum contribution amounts. The 25% of income limit mentioned earlier is not figured out of gross revenue, but from net profits. Besides this, deductions on the half of self employment tax have to be first taken off of the net profit number before the limit for maximum contributions can be accurately determined off of the net profits.

Shareholders

Shareholders are companies, people, or institutions which own minimally a single share of the stock in a given company. They can also be referred to as stockholders. These stockholders are not only investors, but also the owners of the corporation. As owners, they gain the advantageous results from the firm's success. This can translate into higher stock prices, dividend payouts, or hopefully both. Should the corporation not perform well, the stock holders can similarly lose value in their investments as the stock price goes down.

There is a difference between shareholders and owners of partnerships and sole proprietorships. The stakeholders in corporations do not experience personal liability for the financial and debt obligations of the corporation. Should the company in question fail, creditors can not attempt to secure payments or assets from the stockholders as they might be able to do from owners of entities which are privately held.

Corporations with shareholders have another important difference from other structures of businesses. They depend on their executive management and board of directors to handle the day to day operations. This means that the stock holders do not have much control over the daily operations of the company.

Shareholders may not have much involvement in the company's decisions, but they still have important rights. These are specified by the corporation's bylaws and charter. One of these is the right to go through the company records and financial books. Another is to sue the company for officer and director committed mistakes. Even common stock holders have the right to vote on important corporate decisions like whether to agree to a potential merger or on the makeup of the board of directors.

Shareholders have what may be their most important right when a company goes into liquidation through dissolution or bankruptcy. They have the rights to regain a representative amount of the recovered proceeds. They are in line after the secured debt holders including bondholders, preferred stock holders, and creditors, all of whom have precedence over the common stockholders.

Stock holders have several other rights which they enjoy. They receive a part of dividends which their company announces. They also gain the privilege to attend in person the annual meeting of the corporation. Here they are able to learn more regarding the performance of the firm. They can also choose to sit in on the meeting using a conference call. If these common stock holders are not able to or interested in going to the annual meeting, they can instead choose to vote through the mail or online using a vote by proxy. All of these rights which belong to preferred and common shareholders are detailed in the corporate governance policy.

A great number of corporations elect to create two classes of stock. These are common and preferred shares. The majority of stock holders purchase and hold common stocks since they are more of them and they are less expensive than preferred shares. Unlike preferred stock holders who are due to receive dividends every quarter, common shareholders must wait on the board of directors to decide if and when they will be paid a dividend in a given quarter. The directors must decide if this is an appropriate way to utilize the corporation's funds.

Preferred stockholders lack the voting rights of common shareholders. They do receive higher dividends on a more frequent basis. Their payments have to be paid at least yearly and their dividends are also guaranteed. For investors more interested in creating a reliable annual income from investments, preferred shares can be a very helpful tool.

Simple IRA

Among the stable of various types of IRAs American savers for retirement can take advantage of is a less common plan called the SIMPLE IRA. These kinds are a combination of traditional IRAs and employer offered plans like 401(k)s. The word SIMPLE in this case is actually an acronym that stands for Savings Incentive Match Plan for Employees. This is the most common name for the employer offered tax deferred retirement savings account.

SIMPLE IRAs were created to help smaller employers who have 100 or less employees. The idea was for them to offer their workers retirement plans. The IRS knew that the bigger packages of benefits all too often involved long and difficult opening procedures with mountains of complicated paperwork. Smaller employers simply did not have the time or resource capacity to complete and maintain these types of plans.

Among the advantages of SIMPLE IRAs is that they are not governed by ERISA, the Employee Retirement Income Security Act. This means that they are able to sidestep substantial expenses and significant amounts of paperwork in establishing them. The contributions to these kinds of IRA accounts are also fairly straightforward. Employers must make specific minimum amount contributions to the accounts of the employees.

They can accomplish this by establishing a match program at a minimum of 3% of their employee contributions. Alternatively they might set a 2% of his or her salary flat rate and offer it to every employee who participates.

When employees become part of a company SIMPLE plan, they are basically establishing a traditional IRA via their employing company. A significant disadvantage to these types of IRAs centers on their lower contribution limits. These are less than comparable 401(k) plans or other plans which employers sponsor. The limits amount to $12,500 for a single year in tax years 2015 and 2016.

Rolling over from these types of IRAs is also more complicated. They can not be started without a waiting period first being observed. Once employees start their participation with the plans, they can not do a rollover for generally two years on from their participation dates. The only exception to this rule pertains to transfers between SIMPLE IRAs.

These can be done at any time since they are considered to be a tax free transfer from one trustee to another. In the even of any other type of transfer within the two years waiting period, these are deemed as distributions by the IRS. While most penalties for tax deferred plans are set at 10% withdrawal penalties, these particular IRAs carry a more punishing 25% withdrawal tax penalty.

After the conclusion of the two year time frame, individuals may then move their funds from the SIMPLE plan to a different kind of IRA. The only restriction is that they can not move them to a Roth IRA which is funded with pre-taxed dollars. The current SIMPLE plan as well as the new plan must also allow for the transfer to occur.

As with any kind of retirement plan, early withdrawal penalties apply. If any withdrawals occur before the official retirement age of 59 ½ is attained, the early withdrawal penalties of up to 25% will be assessed against the account withdrawals.

When rollovers are done, direct rollovers are much preferred to indirect rollovers. If account holders pursue indirect rollovers there are tax withholding requirements. It is also possible that the account owner will inadvertently fail to complete the transfer in time or at all and then suffer from the substantial early withdrawal tax penalties of up to 25%.

Social Security

Social Security in the United States refers to the federal government's OASDI Old Age, Survivors, and Disability Insurance program. President Franklin Roosevelt created the first such program and signed the Social Security Act legislation in 1935. The present day law has been amended to include other social insurance and social welfare schemes.

The Social Security program is mostly bankrolled using payroll taxes which are referred to as the FICA Federal Insurance Contributions Act tax. The other legislation on it pertains to self employed people. SECA Self Employed Contributions Act Tax collects their contributions. The Internal Revenue Service collects all of these tax deposits and delivers them to the two Social Security Trust Funds. These are the Federal Disability Insurance Trust Fund and the Federal Old Age and Survivors Insurance Trust Fund. All income paid by salaries to a maximum amount set by law contributes to the payroll tax for these programs. Income that people earn above this limit does not incur additional taxes for the programs. This maximum level of taxable earnings in 2016 amounted to $118,500.

The program provides a basis for economic security for 59 million Americans who are retired, disabled, or the family members of those who are deceased or disabled workers. This number amounts to about one in six Americans who receive money from the program. Of this amount approximately 39 million beneficiaries are retired while the rest are survivors of deceased or disabled workers or disabled people themselves. Around 163 million individual Americans pay these taxes so that the others can receive their monthly benefits. This amounts to around a quarter of families collecting income from the programs.

Social Security proves to be a program based on a pay as you go system. Today's workers contribute taxes into the program so that money can go directly out in the form of monthly income to the recipients. This makes it different from prefunded company pension plans. Prefunded programs collect money in advance of retirement benefits being paid. This way it can be distributed to the workers of today when they retire.

Both workers and employers make contributions to the program. Workers give 6.2 percent of income up to the cap. Employers similarly pay an amount that is matching to arrive at the joint contribution of 12.4 percent of all earnings. Those persons who are self employed must pay for both employer and employee share.

Social Security's finances have a bleak outlook. The Office of the Chief Actuary of Social Security comes up with a "best estimate" on when the fund will run out of money to pay benefits. If Congress makes no changes to the law, then in 2020 the benefits spending will actually surpass the revenues for payroll taxes along with the interest on the funds' securities.

At this point, the fund will start cashing in its Treasury securities it obtained as IOU's for loaning money to other branches of the Federal government. In order for the government to pay these IOU's, they will have to obtain money from one or more of a few different sources. Other spending will have to decrease, taxes will have to rise, or the Treasury will have to borrow additional money by selling more securities. This last choice would increase the already high Federal debt.

By 2034, all the assets of the trust fund would have been completely exhausted. This means that all Treasuries the fund has would have been redeemed. By this point, the combined workers and employers taxes would be enough to cover 79 percent of currently promised benefits to recipients. The last year of the 75 years projection shows that by 2089, the payroll taxes would be sufficient to cover around 74 percent of currently promised benefits.

Solo 401(k) Plan

Solo 401(k) plans function much as their standard 401(k) plan cousins do, but display some important differences. These retirement savings plan vehicles for the self employed are also called One Participant 401(k)s, Self Employed 401(k)s, Individual 401(k)s, and Uni-Ks.

These particular 401(k)s provide business owners and spouses who do not have any employees beyond themselves with the ability to be a part of a 401(k) type of tax deferred plan. The plans are fairly new. Congress unveiled them as part of their 2001 Economic Growth and Tax Relief Reconciliation Act. At the time, these became the first specially tailored employer sponsored retirement plans intended for the self employed. Before their introduction, these self employed persons could only rely on such plans as IRAs, Keogh Plans, or Profit Sharing Plans.

These Solo 401(k)s possess practically identical requirements and rules as do the normal 401(k) plans. There are two important exceptions to this. The owner and the business do not find themselves governed by the expensive and complicated requirements of the ERISA Employee Retirement Income Security Act. Besides this, the company is not permitted to employ additional employees who are full time workers contributing 1,000 hours or more each year to the business.

Contributions also have their own particular rules with these Solo plans. The account owner is also both the employee and employer. For the 2016 tax year, employee contributions are limited to $18,000 (or $24,000 per year in the case of those who are fifty years of age or older). Other contributions can be put in as employer contributions. Whichever type a business owning participant wants to call these contributions, the limit for both employee and employer contributions may not be more than $53,000 for a given year.

One benefit that holders of these Solo 401(k) plans enjoy is that they do not have to employ a custodian as with IRAs. Instead they can work with practically any financial institution or bank as their account trustee. Assuming that the trustee will handle it, these plans are able to invest in a wide range of alternative asset types. This includes mutual funds, individual bonds and stocks, ETFs, CDs, real estate, life insurance, S corporations, and precious metals bullion such as gold or silver. Solo Plans are almost unique in their ability to invest in life insurance, which even the self directed IRA plans are not enabled to do.

This all makes the Solo 401(k)s practically unrivalled in their capability to provide retirement plans with low costs, that are easy to make transactions in, with great flexibility, and with generous contribution limits all at once. The downsides to the Solo 401(k) are two. Most workers are not allowed to participate with them. They also need a great deal of paperwork and account maintenance when measured up against numerous other types of retirement plans.

Rollovers are easy to do with these Solo plans. They are able to receive such transfers from other kinds of accounts and IRAs. Account holders may also transfer or roll them over to another kind of retirement account. It is important to check with the rules of an individual's particular plan, as some plans do not accept rollovers from the Solo 401(k)s. Besides this, there are Solo 401(k)s that specifically do not permit rollovers.

Business owners should take care when setting up these types of accounts. Rolling over these types of retirement vehicles will not incur any IRS tax penalties, so long as they are done according to the IRS rules and regulations. An individual has 60 days to finish the procedure and may only engage in it one time per year. Failing to abide by these rules will incur regular income taxes plus the 10% penalty for early withdrawals, unless the individual is older than the 59 ½ years retirement age.

Stocks

Stocks are financial instruments that are issued by publicly traded corporations. These shares of stocks prove to be the tiniest portion of ownership that you can acquire in a company. Even by owning a single share of a company's stock you are a small part owner of the firm.

Owning shares of stock gives you the privilege of voting for the underlying company's board of directors, along with other critical issues that the company is considering. Should a company decide to distribute earnings to share holders as dividends, then you will get a portion of them.

With the ownership of stock, your liability in the company is only limited to the value of your shares. This means that should a company lose a lawsuit and be forced to pay an enormous fine or judgment, then you can not be made to contribute to it. The company's creditors also can not pursue you if the company runs into financial trouble and goes bankrupt.

Two different types of stock shares exist. These are common shares and preferred shares. The vast majority of shares that are issued are common stock shares. These are the shares that members of the public hold most of the time. They come with full voting rights and also the possibility of receiving dividends that the company pays out.

Preferred stocks come with fewer voting rights but give preferential treatment for dividend payment. Preferred stock issues are paid out before common share dividends. Companies that offer preferred stock typically pay dividends on both classes of shares anyway. Preferred stocks also have a higher claim on the assets of a company if it fails.

Liquidity is a feature of stocks that should always be considered. Common stock shares are almost always more liquid than are preferred shares. Large companies offer the greatest amount of liquidity in the trading of their stocks. Because of the depth of the stock markets, you are able to purchase and sell the shares of practically all companies that are publicly traded at any time that the exchanges are working.

When you purchase a stock, you are looking for two different kinds of gains.

Cash flow or passive income with stocks comes from the dividends that they declare and pay out. Capital gains appreciation is realized when you buy a stock at a lower price than the price that you get when you later sell it. While cash flow dividends are smaller payments that are realized on a generally quarterly basis, capital gains turn out to be larger one time returns made when you sell the underlying stock shares investment. At this point, you would no longer own the stock and you would have to purchase another stock in order to work towards cash flow gains from dividends, as well as other possible capital gains.

Tax Bracket

A tax bracket refers to a certain income range against which the government levies a specific income tax rate. With the majority of income taxing systems in the world today, lower incomes fall under lower income rates tax brackets. At the same time, higher incomes are taxed at greater rates. The idea behind such brackets is to ensure that a progressive income tax system remains in place.

In the tax year for 2016, the Internal Revenue Service decreed there would be seven different tax brackets. Each of these offers minute variations on the theme for married filers, single filers, and head of household filers. This led to the de facto establishment of 21 real tax brackets for the tax year.

Importantly, the tax bracket thresholds did increase a little for tax year 2016. As an example, the lowest bracket proves to be under $9,325 for individual taxpayers, which was raised from $9,275 back in tax year 2015. The highest possible tax bracket for this tax year 2016 is now $418,041, itself raised from the 2015 tax bracket high of $415,051. This changes every year, so it is important to consult the IRS.gov website for current information annually.

Those individuals whose incomes are under the minimum bracket of $9,275 have income which is taxed according to the minimum 10 percent tax rate. For everyone filing singly who earns over this amount, the first $9,275 becomes taxed at the rate of 10 percent. Earnings which exceed this on up to $37,650 are then taxed at 15 percent. From $37,650 to $91,150 the earnings become taxed at a steeper 25 percent rate. Income beyond the $91,150 is taxed at still higher rates. This means that many tax filers actually fall into several tax brackets and not only the first one.

The tax bracket should never be confused with the tax rate. Tax rates represent the actual percentage at which the given income becomes taxed. All tax brackets possess their own unique tax rates. Many people simplify and call their tax rates the bracket at which they are taxed as if they were identical. The comparison is not valid since the majority of Americans have earnings which fall into more than one tax bracket.

An example helps to make the tax bracket concept clearer. Consider an individual who earns a hefty $500,000 every year. At such a lofty level as this, the filer will have income that goes into each of the single filing tax brackets. This means the person will pay many different tax rates (seven in fact). This will depend on which part of his or her income is being considered. On all earnings which exceed $406,751 the tax rate will be a punishing 39.6 percent. On the initial $9,075, the rate will merely be the 10 percent rate of the first tax bracket. This means that the actual tax rate of such an individual will lie somewhere in the middle of the two tax rate extremes of 10 percent and 39.6 percent, making it closer to 25 to 35 percent effectively.

The opposite of such a progressive income tax system as this one is a flat tax system. In these taxing arrangements, every individual becomes taxed on all income at the identical rate. It does not matter how much people make in this type of tax setup.

Those analysts and economists in favor of the tax bracket system in particular and progressive tax systems in general argue that the people who make higher incomes can bear a heavier taxing burden and still enjoy a comfortable, high standard of living. Lower income earners will struggle to cover their basic human needs at any tax rate.

The other argument is that such a system will cushion and stabilize against losses in after tax income. The reason is because a real salary decrease becomes counterbalanced out by a drop in the effective tax rate. In this way, people who suffered a pay cut would feel the blow to their post-tax income less severely since the tax rates would drop alongside the income decline.

It is worth noting that such tax brackets do not only apply to individuals who file their income taxes. The IRS also sets the rates and brackets for trusts, companies, and corporations. They adjust both these and the personal tax brackets for the impacts of inflation from time to time.

Tax Deductions

Tax Deductions prove to be a legal method for reducing income which the taxing authorities consider to be taxable. They typically arise because of expenses, especially such costs as taxpayers or businesses experience in the course of producing income or earning profits. This differs from exemptions and credits as both exemptions and deductions actually reduce the amount of income which can be taxed, while the credits applied actually reduce the total tax individuals and business will have to pay.

Two categories into which tax professionals often divide tax deductions are above the line and below the line. Above the line deductions benefit all taxpayers regardless of how much income they earn. Below the line ones only provide value if they surpass the individual taxpayers' standard deductions. For 2016, this deduction turned out to be $6,400 for single taxpayers without families or dependents.

Tax deductions also differ according to business and personal types. For the United States, (as well as most business taxing jurisdictions), businesses may take both trade and business expenses off of their taxable income. These allowances vary widely from one type to another and are often restricted. In order to be permissible, said expenses have to be realized in the operations of the business on an activity the owners undertake in an effort to make profits.

Cost of goods sold is a nearly universally accepted tax deduction for most every system of income tax regardless of the jurisdiction. This reduces the gross income, and tax authorities typically consider it to be an expense. In the United States, the Internal Revenue Service permits "all the ordinary and necessary expenses paid or incurred during the taxable year in carrying on any trade or business" as typical business tax deductions. These will be governed by any applicable limitations, enhancements, and qualifications.

Limitations do exist with regards to these types of business deductions. This is the case even though the necessary expenses may pertain directly to the business in question. Some of these limitations apply to activities which include lobbying expenditures, key employees' compensation packages, the use of vehicles, and entertainment related to the business. Besides this, deductions which exceed the income of one enterprise can not necessarily offset income earned in other ventures. The U.S. limits those deductions from one passive activity to being used against income from another such passive activity.

Depreciation is another key tax deduction which the U.S. permits businesses and sole proprietors. This mechanism for cost recovery happens through deductions in the form of depreciation. It applies to most any tangible asset. The IRS permits such depreciation throughout the potential useful life of the asset, which they estimate.

The government assigns most depreciation (useful life) time-frames using the nature and utilization of such assets and the type of business as their guidelines. For example, they may allow three years of depreciation for tax deductions on a laptop or desktop computer. This means that the cost of the purchase can be divided by three and each resulting third of the price may be used as a specific tax deduction for three consecutive years.

Personal deductions are the other principal type of tax deductions. These pertain to individual taxpayers. Some intrinsically personal goods, costs, or services may be deducted from taxable income, per the IRS. The standard and set allowance for taxpayers and also some of their family members or dependents which they support is determined by the Internal Revenue Service and varies most every year.

The IRS calls these personal exemptions. In the United Kingdom and other British English-speaking jurisdictions throughout the world, these are known as personal allowances. In both types of systems, such exemptions and allowances become reduced and finally eliminated for those married couples or individuals whose income surpasses preset maximum levels.

Among the types of personal exemptions (which the U.S. and many other systems allow) are property taxes and local or state income taxes paid, medical costs, primary home loan interest charges, contributions to charitable organizations, contributions to either health savings or retirement savings plans, and some educational costs or interest paid on education-related student loans. The U.S. and Britain also allow payments to other individuals to become deducible in many cases, such as with child support or alimony.

Tax Exemptions

Tax exemptions are special monetary exemptions that decrease the amount of income which is taxable. This can take the form of full tax exempt status that delivers 100 percent relief from a certain form of taxes, partial tax on certain items, or reduced tax rates and bills. Tax exemption can refer to particular groups such as charitable outfits (who receive exemption from income taxes and property taxes), multi-jurisdictional businesses or individuals, and even military veterans.

The phrase tax exemption is commonly utilized to refer to specific scenarios where the law lowers the amount of income that would fall under the taxable label otherwise. With the American Internal Revenue Service, there are two kinds of exemptions which are available to individuals. One example of a tax exemption concerns the decrease in taxes the IRS gives for any dependent children who are under age 18 (who actually live with the head of household income tax filer).

For the year 2015, the Internal Revenue Service permitted individuals who were filing taxes to receive a $4,000 exemption on every one of their permitted tax exemptions. This simply means that any individuals paying taxes who count on three permissible exemptions are able to deduct fully $12,000 off of their taxable income level.

In the cases where they make a higher amount than an IRS pre-determined threshold, the amount in tax exemptions which they are able to utilize becomes phased out slowly and finally eliminated completely. For the tax year 2015, those individuals filing taxes who earned in excess of $258,250, as well as those married filing jointly couples who earned more than $309,900, received a lower amount for their exemptions. This complicated sliding scale with seemingly random numbers in place is all part of the reason why observers claim the American tax system is outdated and overly complex.

There is an important caveat for individuals filing taxes. They can not claim their own personal exemption when someone else claims them as a dependent on their tax return. This is one of the elements that separate exemptions from deductions in the world of tax terminology. Each individual filing is permitted to claim his or her personal deduction.

Looking at a real world example helps to clarify the complicated rules. Young college students who have a job while they go to school will typically be claimed by their parents like a dependent on the parents' income tax return. Since the parents are claiming them as a dependent, the students are not permitted to claim their own personal exemption. They can take the standard deduction however. This means that the students who earn $13,000 will be allowed to take the $6,300 standard deduction. This lowers their taxable income to $6,700. If their parents did not claim them, it would mean they were able to also claim the personal exemption, which would reduce their taxable earnings down to $2,700 (derived by subtracting the $4,000 exemption amount from $6,700).

In the majority of cases, individuals who file are also able to obtain a personal deduction for their husbands or wives. This does not apply if the spouse turns out to be claimed by their parents as a dependent on the parents' tax return.

There are many scenarios where the dependents of an income tax filer prove to be minor aged children of the primary taxpayer. Regardless of this fact, individuals who pay their taxes may also have other kinds of dependents they can claim for exemption purposes against their income. These dependents are typically relatives of the payer in question, such as a child, parent, sister, brother, uncle, or aunt. They must be truly dependent on the person paying the taxes in order to live for the IRS to accept them as dependents for income tax filing purposes.

It is possible for a person to have no tax liability whatsoever thanks to the combination of personal deductions, personal tax exemptions, and exemptions and deductions for his or her dependents. When this is the case, these individuals are allowed to request an official exemption from withholding tax from their employers. When they do so, their payroll department will only withhold Social Security and Medicare contributions (but not income tax contributions) from their paychecks.

Tax Refund

A Tax Refund refers to money which the IRS Internal Revenue Service gives back to a tax payer for overpayment of their taxes in a given tax year. For the eight out of ten Americans who receive them most every year, they evoke feelings of wild celebration. The truth of the matter is it simply means that this majority overpaid their income tax out of their payroll tax withholding with their employer throughout the calendar year. This is not a good thing in reality.

Self-employed people will also receive a refund if they have overpaid their estimated taxes. This does not represent free money or additional income when a tax check arrives in the mail or is alternatively direct deposited. Instead, it signifies that the recipient cheerfully agreed to loan Uncle Sam money without charging him any interest for the service.

It is also possible for tax refunds to be issued out of refundable tax credits. This can occur if any money remains from such credits after the taxes due from the federal income have been covered. After the federal government receives and processes all of the return for the tax year in question, it must formally sign off on a refund before the money will be dispatched.

The amount of time that this requires varies according to the means which individuals employ in filing their taxes. Electronically filed taxes-refund processing times are usually sent in under 21 days from the Internal Revenue Service accepting the return. It is possible for delays to hinder this by as much as 12 weeks, though it is highly unlikely that this would happen. Paper tax returns which are mailed typically take from six to eight weeks to be issued and arrive in the mail in the form of a traditional paper check.

If individuals wait until peak tax return season to file, their refunds will commonly be delayed. Tax preparers at the IRS can and do become overwhelmed as easily as any person at this busy time of the year. After all, the IRS is not guaranteeing the time frame for the refunds to be sent out, only estimating their best guess. This is why those waiting for a tax refund should never wait on such a payout to fund a critical purchase or make a time sensitive payment (on a house, mortgage, or other credit card bill).

For those who do find themselves in desperate straits to receive such a refund though, there are loans against imminent refunds which taxpayers can apply for and receive. Some tax preparers, such as H&R Block, will issue refunds against owed refunds as well, in exchange for a small percentage convenience fee. All delay liabilities then transfer to the tax preparing firm and away from the individual tax filer.

Where electronic tax refunds are concerned, individuals have three choices. They can have the IRS deposit them to a checking account, savings account, or retirement account (such as an IRA). Besides this, one could have the IRS purchase a $5,000 or less Series I savings bond if he or she fancies receiving less than a single measly one percent per year in interest.

People have up to three years from the point of filing to claim their refund. This means that now in 2017, filers could still apply for a refund from the tax year 2014. When the IRS grants an extension for any reason, the deadline for the three years starts at the end of the deadline extension.

The sad news is that sometimes people are not allowed to keep their whole refund. The IRS could make a tragic mistake and overpay a refund. They will get this back eventually one way or the other. Any individuals who owe back payments on child support will also have this seized, as they would for back taxes of overdue student loan bills. It is also possible to get a smaller than expected check. In the event that the remaining money does not show up within two weeks of the incorrect amount, it is always a recommended idea to contact the Internal Revenue Service directly.

Term Life Insurance

Term life insurance is a form of life insurance. It offers coverage for a preset and limited amount of time that is called the relevant term. The coverage provided is a fixed rate of payment coverage. Once the term expires, the individual's coverage at the rate of the premiums that were charged before are not assured any more.

The client will be forced to drop their term life insurance coverage or to get a different coverage with varying payments and terms. Should the person who is insured die within the term, the death benefit amounts are paid out to the insured person's beneficiary. This term life insurance proves to be the most affordable means of buying a major dollar value of death benefit coverage based on the premium cost charged.

Term life insurance turns out to be the first type of life insurance created, and it stands in contrast to permanent forms of life insurance like universal life, whole life, and variable universal life. These coverage types promise an individual pre set premiums that can not go up for the person's entire life. People do not usually employ term insurance for strategies involving charitable giving or their needs for estate planning. Instead, they are thinking about a need to replace an income if a person passes away on his or her family unexpectedly.

A great number of the permanent life insurance policies also offer the advantage of increasing in value during the person's contract. This cash value can then be withdrawn when certain conditions are met by the policy holder. Generally, withdrawing these cash amounts closes out the policy. Beneficiaries of permanent life insurance products get the insurance policy face value but not the cash value upon the holder's death. Because of this, financial advisers will suggest that people purchase term life insurance for their insurance needs and then invest the money saved over permanent products in retirement accounts that provide tax deferred contributions and investment gains, like 401k's and IRA's.

Like with the majority of insurance policies, term life insurance pays out claims for the insured, assuming that the contract is current and the premiums are paid as due. Assuming that a claim is not filed, the premium is not given back to the policy holder. This makes term life insurance like home owners' insurance policies that pay claims if a home becomes destroyed or damaged as a result of fire, or like car insurance policies that pay drivers if they have a car accident. Premiums are not refunded when the product is no longer required. Because of this, term life insurance like these other products only provides risk protection.

Thrift Savings Plan

The Thrift Savings Plan represents a government created retirement savings vehicle. In 1986, Congress passed the Federal Employee Retirement System Act. This plan was established for the benefit of retired or present employees in the civil service of the federal government.

In 2001, Congress expanded the TSP so that it would include the members of the armed forces with the National Defense Authorization Act. This extended participation beyond the original civilian employees. Armed forces members were allowed to enroll beginning on October 9th of 2001.

The Thrift Savings Plan was set up to be a defined contribution plan. The goal behind its creation was to provide the federal government employees with similar retirement savings types of benefits as private sector workers had. Employees in the private sector already enjoyed these retirement savings opportunities via the available 401(k) plans. With every payroll check, plan contributions to both the 401(k) and TSP are deducted automatically.

These TSPs include a variety of different funds. Participants can choose from and invest in six different types. Among these are the government security fund, the common stock fund, the fixed income fund, the international stock fund, the small cap stock fund, and the life cycle fund.

The government security TSP fund is specifically managed by the Federal Retirement Thrift Investment Board itself. This fund's management purchases U.S. government guaranteed Treasury securities that are not marketable. Because of this conservative and safe strategy, the G Fund does not lose money. Its returns are also lower as a result of this low risk.

The common stock fund is one of the index funds that track a particular benchmark. In the case of this C fund, it invests in a stock index fund which mirrors the composition of the Standard and Poor 500 Index (S&P 500). This means it buys an index based on the various stocks of the 500 medium to larger sized American corporations. Its goal is to replicate the S&P 500s annual performance.

With the fixed income fund, it also tracks a benchmark index. This F fund's goal is to match the Barclays Capital US Aggregate Bond Index's performance. This broad based index was established to represent the bond market in the United States. As such it returns earnings commiserate with American corporate bond performances.

As the name implies, the international stock fund buys prominent stocks of international companies. It also follows a benchmark index. This particular I fund tracks the MSCI Europe, Australasia, Far East Index also known as the EAFE. Its returns are made up of gains or losses from the stock prices, income from dividends, and fluctuations in the comparative currency valuations. Regardless of what is happening in international markets, this fund and the fixed income, common stock, and small cap stock funds are always fully invested.

The small cap stock fund buys the index fund of stocks which follows the Dow Jones US Completion Total Stock Market Index. This S Fund earnings come from both dividend income received and any losses or gains in the prices of the underlying stock.

An interesting combination is the life cycle fund. These are managed to invest in the five different TSP funds. They professionally determine the allocations and percentages in each based on the retirement time frame set by the owner. There are L2020, 2030, 2040, and 2050 versions which assume that within a few years of those dates the owner will be looking to retire and be more conservatively invested.

TSP benefits are several. Government agencies are able to match employee contributions. They also have an agency automatic contribution option. Employees can make catch up contributions when they reach a certain age. These funds feature low, affordable expense ratios. All contributions made to these plans are not taxed until the point where the money is withdrawn at retirement.

Trust

A Trust proves to be a special type of fiduciary arrangement where one participant the trustor grants the other participant the trustee the rights to possess the property title or assets title for the advantages of the beneficiary, often times a third party. When it is utilized in the world of finance, this similarly refers to a kind of closed end investment fund collectively established as a public limited company.

Settlors ultimately establish such trusts. They elect to shift over all or a portion of their possessions (assets) to the trustees of the trust in this action. It is the trustees who ultimately maintain the assets on behalf of the beneficiaries of said trust. The trusts' rules come down to the particular terms that apply to the given trust in question. Some jurisdictions allow for older members of the beneficiaries' class to ascend to the roles of trustee. Some of these jurisdictions actually allow for the grantor to be both a trustee and lifetime beneficiary together at once.

Two different types of trusts exist, the testamentary trust and the living trust. The testamentary trusts are also known as will trusts. These determine the means in which the assets for the individuals will be allocated after they eventually pass away. The document of such a trust comes into play legally following the death of the testator.

On the other hand, living trusts are known as inter vivos or revocable trusts. These written out documents allow for the assets of an individual to be created in the form of a trust. The individual himself or a beneficiary will then enjoy the advantages of and utilization of the resources throughout their remaining lives. Such assets will eventually be transferred to the legal beneficiaries when the individual dies. The trust creator sets a successor trustee who will carry the responsibility of transferring any remaining assets over to the beneficiary in question.

There are a number of different reasons that individuals employ trusts. One of these is to attain a degree of privacy. Wills and their arrangements are often public domain material in many jurisdictions. Trusts can specify the identical conditions which a will may, without the intrusive nature of being public domain documents available for any and all members of the public to read upon demand. This explains why those people who do not wish to have their wills and terms of their estate disposition revealed publically after they are gone will often choose to utilize trusts for their final bequests instead of the will document.

Besides this, trusts are a useful vehicle for planning the payment of taxes. Trusts have different tax arrangements than do standard planning accounts and competing vehicles. The tax consequences for deploying such trusts are typically less negative and expensive than those of other typical means involved in financial planning. This helps to explain why using trusts has become a standard option in the world of efficient tax planning. This is the case not only for individuals but also for corporations.

Finally, trusts find extensive utilization in estate planning procedures. This allows for the assets of deceased people to be passed on to their spouses. The spouses are then able to equally divide up the remaining assets for the benefit of the children who survive the deceased parent. Those children who do not possess the necessary 18 years of age to be considered legal persons (with possession rights) will be required to have trustees to exercise control over all assets in question until they reach the legal age of adulthood.

Universal Basic Income (UBI)

Universal basic income (UBI) is known by a variety of names in different countries and continents. Among the more popular are basic income, citizen's income, unconditional basic income, basic income guarantee, universal demo grant, and UBI. This represents a type of social security welfare program and safety net. In it, all residents or citizens of a nation periodically receive an amount of money which the government or another public institution gives them unconditionally. They receive this on top of and regardless of any other income they earn from work or investment returns. When the money is given out to any persons who live with less than the government-mandated poverty line, it is also known as partial basic income.

This universal basic income and its distribution systems could be financed by the revenues and turnover of publically owned enterprises. These are many times referred to as a citizen's dividend or a social dividend. Such a strategy is a component of a market socialism model, as opposed to market capitalism in which participants' incomes are based on their abilities, hard work, and opportunities. Taxation is another means of paying for such basic income schemes.

It was Thomas Paine's _Agrarian Justice_ published in 1795 where he wrote about capital grants to be provided at the age of majority that began the debates concerning universal basic income within the United States. Up through the year 1986, the phrase which referred to this basic income concept most commonly was "social dividend." After that year, the universal basic income wording gained universal appeal. There are many well-known proponents of the social and economic philosophy. Among them are Ailsa McKay, Philippe Van Parijs, Hillel Steiner, Andre Gorz, Guy Standing, and Peter Vallentyne.

In the United States, this Universal Basic Income has been discussed on a number of different occasions as a serious idea for public policy. The numbers which have been bandied about for Americans amount to approximately $1,000 per month, which would be sent via check to every American. Among the conservatives who espoused the concept and argued for it to be implemented were legendary Nobel prize-winning economist Milton Friedman and former Republican President Richard Nixon.

The base case for this Universal Basic Income has been most effectively argued and written extensively about by Andy Stern, who was once the Service Employees International Union president and who serves as a Columbia University professor since then. He published a book called _Raising the Floor_ in which he argued dramatically and effectively for the UBI.

Stern argues that the concept of a basic guaranteed income has become more necessary for two reasons. On the one hand, the wars on poverty programs have not been so effective nationally. On the other, the rapid advance of technology has led to unparalleled job dislocation and disruption for millions of American workers. This program would deliver an effective floor, or social safety net, to every American.

Critics of the plan in the U.S. have asked how the Federal Government would possibly afford to pay for this proposed program. Stern referenced the 126 existing separate government programs which each already distribute money to American citizens. Some of these might be rolled into the Universal Basic Income program. Besides this, additional taxes would have to be introduced in order to make the proposal a reality. Economists have predicted that implementing such a UBI would require around $3 trillion each year in funding.

Despite the fact that this concept has many critics, it is also possibly the only significant ideology in the early twenty-first century which has supporters on both the right and the left sides of the political, economic, and social spectrum.

The Swiss were given a vote on the UBI issue for their own country in the late spring of 2016, and they soundly rejected it. Interestingly though, the same voters answered an exit poll claiming they expected to see this policy implemented in Switzerland within the next 25 years.

Virtual Digital Currency

A Virtual Digital Currency is a form of money which is completely separate from physical cash, like coins or banknotes. What makes it a currency is that it does bear certain similar characteristics to the physical currencies. Its advantage is in the fact that borderless transfer and instant transactions become possible through it. Crypto currencies and virtual currencies are both considered to be forms of digital currencies.

Such forms of money can be utilized to purchase literal goods and services, though the purely virtual ones are often limited to specific economic systems such as social networks or online gaming communities. Another definition for Virtual Digital Currency is an Internet-based medium of exchange which permits instant and borderless transfers of ownership of real world goods and services.

As a going concern, these Virtual Digital Currency units are relatively new. Their origins lie in the heady dot come bubble heyday of the 1990s. Among the very first of these digital currencies proved to be E-gold. This currency was actually a technologically revolutionized version of a gold standard that arose in 1996. It had the backing of tangible real gold underlying it.

Liberty Reserve was another relatively early comer to the world of virtual currencies in 2006. It allowed participants to convert dollars and Euros into Liberty Reserve Dollar and Euros. Both could be exchanged back and forth without restrictions, hassles, or government regulation for a reasonable one percent charge. The two services had centralization and were heavily utilized by money laundering operations. It was inevitable that the United States Federal government would shut them down in time.

Another form of Virtual Digital Currency known as Q coins or QQ coins was so effective in China after it arose in 2005 that it created a destabilizing impact on the official Chinese exchange of the Yuan currency, thanks to speculators. These digital coins came from the Tencent QQ messaging platform.

Attention given to crypto currencies renewed the global interest in such Virtual Digital Currencies. Bitcoin the gold standard and best-loved and most traded of them came about in 2009. It has since evolved into the most heavily accepted and best-respected of the various crypto currencies.

Several of the respected international central banks and settlement bodies of the world have waded into the murky waters of these digital virtual currencies in recent years. The European Central Bank issued a report in February of 2015 entitled "Virtual currency schemes – a further analysis." This claimed that such virtual currencies were actually digital representations of value which are not issued or guaranteed by any central bank, institution of credit, or e-money authority. The report claimed that in some instances, these virtual currencies may be employed as an alternative choice to traditional money. The prior ECB report from October of 2012 stated that such virtual currencies were unregulated digital monies that developers issued and oversaw. At the time, the ECB said these were accepted and traded among the various members of specific virtual communities.

The Swiss-based Bank for International Settlements (BIS) also issued its own "Digital Currencies" type of report in November of 2015. They defined digital currencies as assets which are represented in a digital form and which possess at least some characteristics of money. They said that these can be expressed in the denomination of a sovereign currency and overseen by an issuer who is responsible for both issuing and converting the digital money into traditionally accepted cash currencies. This means that digital currency is a representation of electronic money, or e-money, per the BIS report. They determined that any currency which is decentralized or automatically issued and which has its own units of value is a virtual currency.

Visa

Visa Inc. proves to be an enormous American-based multinational financial services operation which is headquartered in Foster City, California. The corporation is a successor company to a pioneer organization in the world of all-acceptance credit cards. Its electronic fund processing and transference occurs all over the inhabited world, typically through the unmatched Visa-branded debit cards and credit cards.

Interestingly enough, unlike many of its smaller competitors, Visa does not issue any of its own cards, establish fees or interest rates for consumers or businesses, or even offer credit to anyone. Instead they simply deliver payment products which are Visa branded to financial institutions that then brand their own credit cards. This allows the third party financial institutions and banks to provide debit cards, credit cards, pre-paid credit cards, and cash accessing programs to their own various clients.

Nielson Report issued a 2015 report that followed the credit card industry. They determined that Visa Inc.'s worldwide network, called Visa Net, handled an incredible 100 billion transactions that year. These had a volume for the year of $6.8 trillion.

Visa maintains operations on every inhabited continent. It is accepted on all 6 continents and most inhabited islands of the world. Their impressive volumes of transactions process through Visa Net. They have two separate fortress-like secure facilities that process these global operations and transactions. These are the Operations Center East, found near Ashburn, Virginia; and the Operations Center Central, found in the area of Highlands Ranch, Colorado. Each of these two key data centers for world finance is massively fortified to protect against any combination of terrorism, crime, cyber-crime, and natural disasters. They are able to function independently of one another. The Visa Inc. company is even able to run them from externally placed utilities in an emergency.

Both of the centers are capable of running as many as 30,000 different transactions at the same time. They can process a staggering 100 billion computations per second. Naturally cyber-security and fraud are major issues to these two financial data center of the world. To this effect, each processed transaction is run against 500 independent variables. Among these are 100 different fraud-detection protocols. Examples of these are the individual spending patterns of the customer involved, the location of the merchant running the transaction, and the geographical location of the customer in question. Only after the 500 variables and 100 fraud protocols pass muster will any single transaction be accepted. This is an unparalleled level of financial security in the realm of credit and debit cards.

The name Visa came from the mind of corporate founder Dee Hock. Hock felt that the word Visa could be recognized around the globe instantly in a number of different languages throughout numerous countries. He believed it gave a connotation of universal acceptance as well.

Back on October 11th of 2006, the company Visa declared that it would merge businesses and transform into a publically held company via an initial public offering. For the restructuring to work as an IPO, Visa decided to merge several of its sister outfits Visa USA, Visa International, and Visa Canada into a single company. Meanwhile, they spun off Visa of Western Europe into an individual standalone company. Its member banks own this European operation and also gained a minority stake in the newly-issued shares of Visa Inc.

The IPO deal was so massive that over 35 different investment banks worked on the offering, many of them as underwriters of this huge Initial Public Offering. This IPO became the single biggest Initial Public Offering in the history of the United States when it initially raised $17.9 billion at once. When the underwriters of the IPO decided to exercise overallotment options, they bought another 40.6 million shares in total. This increased the aggregate number of IPO shares to an astonishing 447 million. The final proceeds amount from the IPO then amounted to $19.1 billion. Today Visa trades on the prestigious New York Stock Exchange NYSE with the stock symbol of V.

Wall Street

Wall Street is a physical street that is seven blocks long and runs from Broadway to the New York East River. It lies to the south of the Manhattan borough of New York City. The street is incredibly significant because it has played host to a number of the most important financial entities in the United States.

The city originally got its name because of an earthen built wall that Dutch Settlers of the city erected in 1653 to ward off an anticipated invasion of the English. The street's importance grew so rapidly that before the Civil War in America this was already known as the nation's sole financial capital. In the district of Wall Street there are many important buildings and headquarters.

The street contains the Federal Reserve Bank, the New York Stock Exchange, the International Commodity, Cocoa, Sugar, Coffee, and Cotton Exchanges, and the NYSE Amex Equities. There are also numerous municipal and government bond dealers, investment banks, trust companies, and insurance and utilities' headquarters located here. A great number of the major American brokerage firms have their headquarters in this financial district.

Because of Wall Street, New York City is sometimes called the most important financial center in the world as well as the greatest and most powerful city economically. Investors find the two biggest stock exchanges in the world as measured by market capitalization here in the NASDAQ and the New York Stock Exchange. A few other significant exchanges also make or made their headquarters here. These are the New York Board of Trade, The New York Mercantile Exchange, and the one time American Stock Exchange.

In the 2000's there were seven major Wall Street firms here. These included Lehman Brothers, Merrill Lunch, Morgan Stanley, Goldman Sachs, Citigroup Inc, JP Morgan Chase, and Bear Stearns. Several of these companies failed outright or had to be sold at urgently distressed prices to rival financial companies in the Great Recession that ran from 2008-2010. Lehman Brothers had to file for bankruptcy in 2008. The U.S. government made JP Morgan Chase buy Bear Stearns. The Treasury and the Federal Reserve then forced Bank of America to purchase Merrill Lynch.

The catastrophic collapse of this many major financial firms dramatically downsized Wall Street with massive re-structuring. It proved to be especially severe for the economies of New York City and the surrounding states. This was because the financial industry in New York produced nearly a quarter of all income in the city. It also amounted to about 10% of all tax revenue for the city and 20% of taxes for the state of New York. City and state government revenues and budgets suffered dramatically from this loss of revenue for years. The Boston Consulting Group estimated in 2009 that as many as 65,000 jobs were permanently gone as a result of the financial crisis.

This city and financial center has grown to become a global symbol for investment and high finance. Movies have been made about it including two with the same title Wall Street and its sequel Wall Street: Money Never Sleeps. The financial district has become a part of modern mythology in many ways starting back in the 1800s.

The street emerged as a hated symbol of the greedy robber barons who took advantage of workers and farmers to the populists of the 19th century. When times were good it represented the way to get rich quick. Following such terrible stock market crashes as 1929 and 2008 the street looked like the home of financial manipulators who could crush major international companies and even derail the economies of entire nations.

Wire Transfer

A wire transfer is the quickest, safest, most reliable means of sending money within the United States, in other countries, or around the world. They are often essential in the more critical financial activities of life such as purchasing a house. The reason larger transactions occur in this form of payment is because the recipient can receive and verify the funds transfer the same day it is done, or as near to immediately as possible (besides Western Union and Money Gram, which cost substantially more to utilize).

A wire transfer actually represents a means to electronically transfer money from one party to another via a bank as intermediary. A traditional and typical wire transfer starts at a credit union or bank and electronically processes through either Fedwire or SWIFT networks. Another common name for such a wire transfer is a bank wire, which also encompasses the standard bank to bank transfers.

Ultimately the wire transfers have become so successful and utilized throughout the United States and rest of world simply because they are capable of moving even enormous sums of money to any destination bank in the world in only a day or two. If they are affected within the same country such as the United States then same day wires can be done. For an international transfer via wire transfer, it often requires another day or even two to complete.

Since the funds move rapidly through the financial system, recipients are not required to wait a material amount of time for the funds to become cleared. This means they can access and utilize the money without significant delays. No holds are typically placed on wire transfer monies. The safety issue means that merchants prefer the wire mechanism. This is because checks can bounce because of insufficient funds, while wires never do so. In other words, these are guaranteed funds.

There are some particular requirements that wire transfers need in order to be possible to transact. At least in the United States, both parties would require a functioning bank account in order for a bank to act as intermediary. Since thieves can not open a bank account too easily, nor bank anonymously in the United States, it is difficult for them to carry out scams using bank wires. This is because it leaves a paper trail which is easy for law enforcement officials to follow.

This does not mean that wire transfer scams are unknown entirely. It is possible for a person to be tricked into wiring money to a fraudster for a purchase or service they never receive. Examples of this are fake insurance policies or false retirement or investment products. Once the wire has cleared the recipients account, they can either withdraw the funds in person or wire it to an offshore overseas account.

By the time the victims realize that they have been scammed, the funds sent by wire will be long gone. They would no longer be recoverable by traditional U.S. law enforcement or even court order methods once they have been transferred offshore. Pulling money back after it has been dispatched via bank wire is extremely difficult in any case. This is true even if the funds remain in the recipient's bank account.

Wire transfer fees can be significant. In many parts of the United States, they run as high as $40 to dispatch a bank wire. Many banks charge upwards of $10 in order for a bank wire to be received into an account. The costs to send one are higher if the wire is funded by utilizing a credit card cash advance. Cash advance fees would then apply, as well as typically large interest rates, plus the wire transfer fee. This is why it is typically most financially sound to effect a bank wire directly from the sender's bank account.

Other books in this Financial IQ Series

Real Estate Terms

Retirement Terms

Banks & Banking Terms

Investment Terms

Accounting Terms

Economics Terms

Mortgage Terms

Stock Trading Terms

Corporate Finance Terms

Small Business Terms

Financial Acronyms

Laws & Regulations

www.ingramcontent.com/pod-product-compliance
Lightning Source LLC
Chambersburg PA
CBHW071549210326
41597CB00019B/3170